SURVIVING

THE

STRETCHING

PASTOR KYLE DRIGGERS

Surviving The Stretching

Copyright © 2021 Kyle Driggers

All rights reserved.

ISBN: 978-1-7363178-4-6

Published by

Shannon LeAnn
—— Unlimited ——
PUBLISHING DIVISION

Table of Contents

INTRODUCTION
The Stretch

It seems that we are living in a time when convenience and comfort are two primary goals of the Christian life. If we are not careful, we will trade off the much-needed areas of discipleship, evangelism, and spiritual discipline for luxury, technology, modern amenities and comfort. A mentality is rising saying "God would never ask me to do something that I am uncomfortable with." Or some think "Surely, He would never require me to do something that I'm not qualified to do."

I find that Biblical faith speaks quite the contrary. Just search the Word of God and you will find that its pages are filled with the stories of men and women that were STRETCHED beyond their comfort zones, beyond their desires, and many times beyond their natural qualifications. The same anointing that was placed upon the vessels used in Scripture is still available to the Church of today. The same divine enablement can be applied to the hearts and lives of believers of our day. If only God's people are willing to SURVIVE THE STRETCHING!

The Bible has been written, recorded, and made available to us by men and women of God that have gone before us. It does not end there! God is still writingthe story of Faith. This story is being recorded upon the minds and hearts of generations that are following in our footsteps. And how do I make my way into this story of Faith? Is it possible for me to do something great for God? Could I be healed or be the recipient of a miracle or some amazing blessing or provision? Absolutely! But first, I must SURVIVE THE STRETCHING!

How do I know if I'm being stretched?

Many times, God begins to stretch us and we resist, thinking that any discomfort or pain must surely be coming from the devil. After all, isn't my life supposed to be better now that I am a Christian? Shouldn't I be smelling roses, walking in the sunshine and feeling the gentle breeze now that I am a believer? While it is true that you become a brand-new creature once you are born again, it is also true that you still live in this contaminated world. You are still going to experience the pressures of life. You are still going to have to work by the sweat of your brow. You are still going to have delivery pains if you give birth to anything. And while the devil is continually active in this present age, it is not true that every struggle and every inconvenience is the work of the devil.

Often, the pressure you are feeling is God merely beginning to stretch you. Shortly after I first preached this message, someone made this remark to me: "Pastor, I'm being stretched! If I didn't know that it was God stretching me, I would think that He was trying to kill me!" That area of your life that has left you feeling abandoned, hopeless and desolate is more than likely the same area that God is trying to stretch you in. Job was talking about this stretching process when he said, *"Though He slay me, yet will I trust him:"* (Job 13:15). Of course, God is not trying to kill you. Like Job, He is allowing the things in your life because He is stretching you. Because Job survived the stretching, he was increased and taken to a new level. Are you ready to go to the next level with God? You must be willing to SURVIVE THE STRETCHING!

Why would God stretch me?

Let me illustrate by saying that I play (or play at) the piano. I remember learning three chords to make it through a song: C chord, F chord, and G chord. I was extremely limited. Some songs had a fourth chord and some people did not sing in the key of C. I soon learned that I had to stretch myself to play for a man that would sing in the key of G. I had to learn new chords and how to play them efficiently. I soon learned most of the chords for the major keys. I thought I was doing good. It wasn't long before I could play for just about any song for any person WITHIN my home Church. I thought I had accomplished something worth bragging about until I was visiting another Church. One of the men there knew me and knew that I played. He called me to the piano to play for the service. I was ready (or so I thought) until the man playing the guitar next to me told me to put it in Ab. I knew how to play in A and I figured there couldn't be much of a difference until he started playing in Ab and I was banging away on the piano in the key of A. Needless to say, I quickly learned that I did not know everything and that there was more to learn. I am still a student and realize that there will always be room to stretch!

I find that serving God is very similar. To be effective, we cannot become stale. We cannot lie down in a rut and think that we are one of God's college professors or military generals. It is not our job to tell everyone else how to do it. We are students in His classroom and as long as we are under His guidance, He will be stretching us to learn more, do more, and be more than we ever thought imaginable. It will be difficult. It will at times be gut-wrenching. It will cost us luxuries and privileges at times. But He is stretching us to become the soldiers that He knows He created us to be!

All for His Glory!

As we explore some of these stories together, it will pay us well to remember that we are created for His pleasure and He deserves ALL the glory! The Twenty-Four Elders around the throne are recorded singing this praise to God: "*Thou art worthy, O Lord, to receive glory and honour and power: for thou hast created all things, and for thy pleasure they are and were created"* (Revelation 4:11). We are not meant to understand everything, and we will not be able to comprehend all of His ways for surely they are higher than ours (Isaiah 55:9). If we will simply trust Him and obey, we will find out that the result is GOOD for us and GLORY for Him!

1 Hear my prayer, O LORD, give ear to my supplications: in thy faithfulness answer me, and in thy righteousness.

2 And enter not into judgment with thy servant: for in thy sight shall no man living be justified.

3 For the enemy hath persecuted my soul; he hath smitten my life down to the ground; he hath made me to dwell in darkness, as those that have been long dead.

4 Therefore is my spirit overwhelmed within me; my heart within me is desolate.

5 I remember the days of old; I meditate on all thy works; I muse on the work of thy hands.

6 I stretch forth my hands unto thee: my soul thirsteth after thee, as a thirsty land. Selah.

7 Hear me speedily, O LORD: my spirit faileth: hide not thy face from me, lest I be like unto them that go down into the pit.

8 Cause me to hear thy lovingkindness in the morning; for in thee do I trust: cause me to know the way wherein I should walk; for I lift up my soul unto thee.

9 Deliver me, O LORD, from mine enemies: I flee unto thee to hide me.

10 Teach me to do thy will; for thou art my God: thy spirit is good; lead me into the land of uprightness.

11 Quicken me, O LORD, for thy name's sake: for thy righteousness' sake bring my soul out of trouble.

12 And of thy mercy cut off mine enemies, and destroy all them that afflict my soul: for I am thy servant.

Psalm 143

Has the enemy persecuted your soul? Do you feel like you have been knocked to the ground? Wandering around in the darkness? Overwhelmed? Distressed? Desolate? Perhaps God is stretching you! Are you willing to stretch your hands to Him? Let's go together and see what happens when we SURVIVE THE STRETCHING!

CHAPTER 1
No More, Forever

We all know someone that is bound and cannot get free from some type of addiction, mindset, or emotional distress. If we are honest, we have all been that someone. If we dare to examine our lives close enough, we may have to admit that there are still things (not necessarily big things) that cling to us and hinder us from fully surrendering to the Lord and His service. The Nation of Israel had a continual struggle with bondage. Possibly, their bondage in Egypt was one of the most depictive stories of how bondage works and how difficult it can be to become free. Difficult but not impossible! As you read this, whatever is binding you, be assured that freedom is possible with God! You may have to do some stretching, but you can and will get free if you SURVIVE THE STRETCHING!

From Guests to Slaves

Israel did not go into Egypt handcuffed and enslaved. No sir, they went in as honored guests. You see, their brother Joseph had been elevated from the pit that they threw him in. He was now Pharaoh's right-hand man. While the rest of the surrounding world was starving during the famine, Egypt was flourishing under Joseph's administration. His father, brothers, and their families all come to Egypt to ride out this famine. They ended up staying too long. Joseph died, and another Pharaoh rose to power *"which knew not Joseph"* (Exodus 1:8). He feared that this fruitful people would have too much power and risked a threat to his kingdom. He established taskmasters over the people to afflict them and burden them down with labor.

One of the hardest things for people to understand about addiction or any type of bondage, is that it never starts drudgingly. It never starts out being burdensome. It may even begin with a thrill or feelings of excitement and ecstasy. It is not perceived as bondage at first! Slowly that thrill or excitement turns into a cruel taskmaster that cannot be escaped! We may go in as guests, but if we dabble too long with the things of this world, we will become enslaved by their grip and afflicted by their consequences. Their time in Egypt totaled 430 years (Exodus 12:40, 41) meaning that generation after generation was afflicted and enslaved simply because they dwelt too long in a place that was not meant to be their home.

Israel stayed in this captive state until God raised up a man that He knew He could stretch! He raised up a man that He knew He could use to get the glory out of Israel's mass departure from their enslaved condition.

Do you realize that God is still raising up men and women to do the same today? He is raising up men and women to set families free! To set communities free! To set Church bodies free! You could be that man or woman, but you must be willing to SURVIVE THE STRETCHING!

Unqualified

I want to be clear where Moses was when God finally got his attention and gave the instructions as to what He wanted Moses to do. He was on the backside of a desert. He was not there for a family retreat. He did not go down there for a camp meeting or to attend a spiritual warfare conference! He was there hiding because he had killed an Egyptian. He knew in his heart that what they were doing was wrong, but he did not know how to handle it. When he handled it his way, he ran for fear of the price that he would have to pay. We can never run so far that God cannot get to where we are. God reveals himself to a murderer and runaway fugitive! How qualified does that sound? It gets even better when Moses himself tells God: *"I am slow of speech, and of a slow tongue"* (Exodus 4:10). In other words, "How can I go back and speak for you when I can barely speak at all? I am unqualified for this job!" Again, God often calls us to do things that go beyond our natural capabilities! He is not looking for skill. He is not looking for talent or giftedness. He is looking for men and women that He can stretch so that He will get the glory!

Despite his lack of qualifications, God in His infinite wisdom still chose Moses to be the man through which He would demonstrate His deliverance. Notice, that while Moses is stretching in obedience, the hand of God is also stretching out to do the miraculous; *"And I will stretch out My hand, and smite Egypt with all My wonders which I will do in the midst thereof: and after that he* (Pharoah) *will let you go"* (Exodus 3:20).

When Moses went before Pharaoh, he is met with resistance as Pharaoh refuses to let the people go. Let's be clear. God could have instantly removed Pharaoh. He could have caused him to fall dead but rather we find that He allows Pharoah to resist. The scriptures tell us that God Himself hardened Pharaoh's heart. Anyone that has ever desperately needed deliverance can relate to this. Instead of receiving instant relief and healing, many times things go from bad to worse once we begin the journey toward freedom. Never forget that God allows what will bring more Glory to Himself. All of this – the hardening of Pharaoh's heart, the Plagues, the Stretching – will be for His Glory!

The Plagues

Out of the ten plagues, six of them have a unique command in them to either stretch out the hand or to stretch out the rod. During these plagues, God was stretching His hand against Egypt for this purpose: *"And the Egyptians shall know that I am the Lord, when I stretch forth mine hand upon Egypt..."* (Exodus 7:5a). The first of the plagues begins after Pharaoh's first refusal to let the people go. God instructs Moses in Exodus 7:19 to *"Say unto Aaron, Take thy rod, and* **stretch** *out thine hand upon the waters of Egypt, upon their streams, upon their rivers, and upon their ponds, and upon their pools of water, that they may become blood; and that there may be blood throughout the land of Egypt, both in vessels of wood and in vessels of stone."* This plague hit Egypt hard as the Nile River supplied not only water but also fish for the Egyptian and Israelite people. The river along with its streams as well as ponds and pools of water were miraculously turned to blood. Water that had been reserved in vessels of wood and stone was also turned to blood. Egypt was now filled with blood. The fish died. The river that once produced life now produced a stench throughout the land (Exodus 7:21). The Egyptians were forced to dig wells to have water to drink (Exodus 7:24). This continued for seven days after the Lord caused Aaron to stretch out his hand.

No doubt this was a time of stretching for the Israeli people as well as the Egyptians as they experienced this plague. They too depended heavily upon the river and its provisions. Many times when we begin to stretch for deliverance, we think that it will come immediately or at least quickly. We feel that there will be no "bloody" issues to deal with, no dry times to endure. We must remember that stretching will be uncomfortable, but it will also be worthwhile!

God would use this same instruction of telling Aaron or Moses to stretch out their hand to bring even more plagues upon the land of Egypt. Look at the following scriptures:

5

*"5 And the LORD spake unto Moses, Say unto Aaron, **Stretch** forth thine hand with thy rod over the streams, over the rivers, and over the ponds, and cause frogs to come up upon the land of Egypt. 6 And Aaron **stretched** out his hand over the waters of Egypt; and the frogs came up, and covered the land of Egypt."*

Exodus 8:5,6

The magicians of Egypt were able to duplicate this act but they were not able to get rid of the frogs so Pharaoh called on Moses and Aaron with a false promise that he would let the people go if they got rid of the frogs. Moses went before the Lord and God caused them to die out of the houses, villages and fields (Exodus 8:13). They were gathered up by the heaps and their stench permeated the land of Egypt (Exodus 8:14).

*"16 And the LORD said unto Moses, Say unto Aaron, **Stretch** out thy rod, and smite the dust of the land, that it may become lice throughout all the land of Egypt. 17 And they did so; for Aaron **stretched** out his hand with his rod, and smote the dust of the earth, and it became lice in man, and in beast; all the dust of the land became lice throughout all the land of Egypt."*

Exodus 8:16, 17

With this plague, God had done something that the Egyptian magicians could not replicate. They tried to convince Pharaoh that this was "the finger of God" but he would not listen. Instead, he hardened his heart

(Exodus 8:19). God would send swarms of flies and pestilence upon the cattle of Egypt. He sent boils upon the people, but Pharaoh continued to harden his heart. He refused to let the people go. The Lord sends Moses early in the morning to stand before Pharaoh and sends a warning: *"For now I will stretch out my hand, that I might smite thee and thy people with pestilence; and thou shalt be cut off from the earth"* (Exodus 9:15). And indeed God would keep His word!

*"22 And the LORD said unto Moses, **Stretch** forth thine hand toward heaven, that there may be hail in all the land of Egypt, upon man, and upon beast, and upon every herb of the field, throughout the land of Egypt. 23 And Moses **stretched** forth his rod toward heaven: and the LORD sent thunder and hail, and the fire ran along upon the ground; and the LORD rained hail upon the land of Egypt."*

Exodus 9:22, 23

This hail would beat upon the men, their homes, their livestock and break down their fields and trees as well. Only the land of Goshen was spared which is where the Israelites stayed (Exodus 9:26). After pleading with Moses and offering yet another broken promise, God stopped the hail and Pharaoh would again harden his heart.

*"12 And the LORD said unto Moses, **Stretch** out thine hand over the land of Egypt for the locusts, that they may come up upon the land of Egypt, and eat every herb of the land, even*

7

*all that the hail hath left. 13 And Moses **stretched** forth his rod over the land of Egypt, and the LORD brought an east wind upon the land all that day, and all that night; and when it was morning, the east wind brought the locusts."*

Exodus 10:12, 13

These locusts filled the land in such a way that the Egyptians had never seen before. They consumed what harvest was left in the fields and what fruit was left in the trees from the devastation of the hail. Pharaoh called for Moses and Aaron again, pleading forgiveness for his sin. The Lord caused a strong west wind to clear the land of the grievous locusts, but He also hardened Pharaoh's heart so that he would again refuse to let the people go. This time, God would do something so tremendous that Pharaoh and the Egyptians would be filled with such fear that they would not get up or leave their dwellings for three whole days. God would turn out the lights in Egypt! For the sixth and final time out of the ten plagues, God would instruct one of His servants to STRETCH!

*"21 And the LORD said unto Moses, **Stretch** out thine hand toward heaven, that there may be darkness over the land of Egypt, even darkness which may be felt. 22 And Moses **stretched** forth his hand toward heaven; and there was a thick darkness in all the land of Egypt three days:"*

Exodus 10:21, 22

This darkness was so thick that the Egyptians could not see one another. They would not even get up because the darkness was so heavy. I am sure that most of us have been in some dark places. Possibly, there have been times that we could not see our hand in front of our face. But I doubt that we have ever been in darkness so thick as what Egypt encountered for these three days. Yet it was still not enough. Pharaoh would have to lose his firstborn son along with every first-born son in Egypt. Even the first born among the cattle would have to die for Pharaoh to consent to Moses' request to be set free (Exodus 12:30). Pharaoh called for Moses and Aaron that same night and told them to *"Rise up, and get you forth from among my people, both ye and the children of Israel; and go, serve the Lord as ye have said"* (Exodus 12:31).

This would mark the end of the plagues but not the end of the "stretching."

A Change of Heart

Moses and the Israelites had not traveled far before Pharaoh's heart was hardened yet again. He along with his servants, horsemen, horse, and chariots go after the Israelites and begin to close in on them close to the Red Sea. God has a remedy that is all too familiar to Moses. He tells Moses in Exodus 14:16 to *"… lift up thy rod, and* **stretch** *out thine hand over the sea, and divide it: and the children of Israel shall go on dry ground through the midst of the sea."*

Deliverance requires both faith and obedience. We must have the faith that God can and will do the supernatural when He considers necessary. We must act in obedience to His Word, even when it may seem foolish or contrary to the natural mind. Moses has proven himself to be a man of both faith and obedience and this time would be no different. Exodus 14:21 records what happened. *"And Moses **stretched** out his hand over the sea; and the Lord caused the sea to go back by a strong east wind all that night, and made the sea dry land, and the waters were divided."* The Israelites needed a miracle and that is exactly what God gave them. *"And the children of Israel went into the midst of the sea upon the dry ground: and the waters were a wall unto them on their right hand, and on their left"* (Exodus 14:22).

This would make for a beautiful ending except for one problem. The Egyptians were still behind them. So many believers stop here in their walk with God and never experience full deliverance. They spend their entire Christian experience running from the devil. He chases them from one temptation to another; one unpleasant situation to another; one failure to the next. They spend so much time looking over their shoulder to see how close the devil is following them that they never get to enjoy what God has placed in front of them. Of course, there will always be temptations. There will always be a need to be aware of the enemy's snare. He will always be a seducer, an accuser, a thief and a murderer. However, we don't have to be controlled by those things. We don't have to be tormented and we don't have to live under a cloud of doubt or fear.

Many Christians do not allow themselves to be stretched until deliverance is clear. They stop when it gets bloody. They stop when things get a little sticky or a little stinky. They stop when things get dark. And then many get to this point and they stop once they feel a little freedom. Israel's deliverance did not happen at the edge of the Red Sea. God has them to do just a little more stretching.

Thus the Lord Saved (Delivered) Israel

Just one more time, God commands Moses to *"stretch out thine hand over the sea, that the waters may come again upon the Egyptians, upon their chariots, and upon their horsemen"* (Exodus 14:26). In full faith and seeing all that God had done thus far *"... Moses **stretched** forth this hand over the sea, and the sea returned to his strength when the morning appeared; and the Egyptians fled against it; and the Lord overthrew the Egyptians in the midst of the sea"* (Exodus 14:27).

Moses had to stretch out one final time and the Lord completely overthrew the Egyptians. My question to you is this: Will you allow yourself to be stretched until you see a complete deliverance from whatever ails you? Or will you settle for what somebody else told you? Will you settle for some secular program for rehabilitation? Will you settle for a warm feeling that you had in Church? My prayer is that you will continue to let God stretch you until you can say like Moses did in Exodus 14:13 *"Fear ye not, stand still and see the salvation of the Lord,*

11

which He will show to you today: for the Egyptians whom ye have seen to day; ye shall see them again no more for ever!"

"Thus the Lord saved (delivered) Israel that day out of the hand of the Egyptians; and Israel saw the Egyptians dead upon the sea shore."

Exodus 14:30

Can you imagine seeing the thing that once held you captive finally defeated and no longer a threat? Can you imagine the relief, the freedom, the liberation that the Israelites felt following that last stretch of Moses' hand? Full deliverance does exist and can be yours if you will SURVIVE THE STRETCHING!

CHAPTER 2
For I Will Give It Into Thine Hand

The life of the Believer is one of victory! Because of who you belong to and because of who you believe in, you already have the victory. This is also a life of possession. What does that mean? We sing about victory and hear sermons about victory, but we do not hear much about possession. This book that we preach out of and have placed our trust in, the BIBLE, is full of promises! It is full of weapons that we may use in our times of battles! It is filled with nuggets of gold that are worth more than money can buy! And they all belong to us if we are daring enough to STRETCH until we possess them and have victory over every area that may keep us back from laying hold on them!

What a blessing to know that we do not have to walk around with our heads held down! We do not have to live with our shoulders stooped and our back bent beneath loads of sorrow and care. We do not have to live under the clouds of doubt and unbelief, constantly fighting the storms of depression, oppression, anxiety and mental fatigue! We do not have to allow sickness or shame or financial set back dictate to us a life of fear, condemnation or shame! We can possess the promises of God and obtain the victorious life offered to us through Christ... if we can SURVIVE THE STRETCHING!

Never Underestimate the Small Things!

The city of Ai should not have been a threat to the people of Israel. In reality, some even felt like they could conquer Ai with very little effort: *"And they returned to Joshua, and said unto him, Let not all the people go up; but let about two or three thousand men go up and smite Ai; and make not all the people to labour thither; for they are but few"* Joshua 7:3. This little place of Ai, that seemed like they were "but few" put Israel on the run! The next verses tell us what happened: *"So there went up thither of the people about three thousand men: and they fled before the men of Ai. 5 And the men of Ai smote of them about thirty and six men: for they chased them from before the gate even unto Shebarim, and smote them in the going down: wherefore the hearts of the people melted, and became as water"* Joshua 7:4,5.

Many Christians know this feeling all too well. We win battle after battle; obtain promise after promise; then, along comes some small problem or obstacle. This small thing should not even cause us to blink but somehow, now we are on the run. Trembling and heartbroken; our faith is shaken because of a small thing. Never underestimate the small things! Disobedience or lack of faith can cause the smallest of obstacles to become the biggest hindrances. If we are not mindful, we will be like Israel: a mighty army running from a small enemy!

The Bible does not give us much room for running. There are times of temptation when we ought to flee or take the way of escape. There are times of weakness when we must recognize our frailty and run back to the source of our strength and power. There times that we have drifted from God and must repent and run back to Jesus as fast as we can! However, when it comes to possessing the promises of God, we as God's children must take a stand. We must learn to quit backing down and to quit running from the enemy!

The Accursed Thing

After the Israelites flee from Ai, Joshua falls on his face before God seeking for an answer. God gives Joshua an answer that I am sure he did not want to hear. God tells Joshua: *"Israel hath sinned, and they have also transgressed my covenant which I commanded them: for they have even taken of the accursed thing, and have also stolen, and dissembled also, and they have put it even among their own stuff"* Joshua 7:11. Joshua had warned the people back at Jericho that the city was accursed along with all that was in it (see Joshua 6:17). Only Rahab and those in her house would be allowed to live because of her faith and willingness to help the spies. He would further warn that anyone that took from that which was accursed would become accursed and cause trouble for the Israelite people (see Joshua 6:18). Only the silver, gold, brass and iron were allowed to be brought into the treasury of the Lord (see Joshua 6:19).

A man by the name of Achan did just what they were warned not to do: he took that which was forbidden and brought the judgment of God on the whole congregation of Israel (see Joshua 7:1). Many times, we fail to realize what sin and disobedience will do for us. It blocks us from the very things that God says we can have. Look at what God says in Joshua 7:12 *"Therefore the children of Israel could not stand before their enemies, but turned their backs before their enemies, because they were accursed: neither will I be with you any more, except ye destroy the accursed from among you."* Sin causes us to tremble in the presence of adversity. Disobedience will always result in us cowering before the enemy. Israel fled and even lost thirty-six men to a city that they were more than equipped to conquer. All because of SIN! And while sin develops a wall between us and God (see Isaiah 59:1,2), there is always hope for redemption and a second chance. God tells Joshua to get up and sanctify (consecrate) the people and to get rid of that which is accursed among the people (see Joshua 7:13).

Joshua follows the Lord's commands and gets rid of the curse from among the people. It cost Achan his life, along with his entire family. Thankfully, we don't have to let disobedience and sin take us this far. On the same note, if we expect to live a victorious life, we do have to destroy and get rid of the things that God calls accursed. Paul admonished the Romans by saying: *"For if ye live after the flesh, ye shall die: but if ye through the Spirit do mortify the deeds of the body, ye shall live"* Romans 8:13. Living to please the flesh leads to defeat and death but the Spirit of God helps us to mortify (put to death) the deeds and acts of the flesh.

Another passage of scripture to consider is Colossians 3:5-10 *"Mortify therefore your members which are upon the earth; fornication, uncleanness, inordinate affection, evil concupiscence, and covetousness, which is idolatry: 6 For which things' sake the wrath of God cometh on the children of disobedience: 7 In the which ye also walked some time, when ye lived in them. 8 But now ye also put off all these; anger, wrath, malice, blasphemy, filthy communication out of your mouth. 9 Lie not one to another, seeing that ye have put off the old man with his deeds; 10 And have put on the new man, which is renewed in knowledge after the image of him that created him:"* Christians have experienced an act of God called regeneration (also referred to as the "New Birth" or "Being Born Again"). In this New Birth, we are transformed and "renewed in knowledge" after the one that created us. But we should never be deceived into thinking that our old nature and the "accursed things" of the flesh won't try to resurface. The enemy will continue to use these "accursed things" to block us from the promises of God and from living victoriously. Let's identify some of the things that Paul listed when he wrote this passage to the Colossians:

- *Fornication* – The Greek word used here can be translated "harlotry" but includes "adultery" and "incest." Very simply put, fornication is any sexual activity with someone that is not your spouse. I would venture to say that this includes not only the "normal" idea of sexual intercourse but includes all types of sexual activity outside of the marriage relationship. I will go a step further and quote what Jesus said in Matthew 5:28 *"But I say unto you, That whosoever looketh on a woman to lust after her hath committed adultery with her already in his heart."* This goes further than the physical and dives even into the mental realm of man (and woman). If a man or woman looks on another with lust (a longing, a desire, to covet), Jesus said he or she has already committed adultery in their heart. Let us be mindful that human beings are sexual creatures and the sexual experience was created by God for both procreation and recreation. With that being said, it is near impossible for a man or woman not to desire some type of sexual attention just as it would be unhealthy for a person to no longer desire food or water. However, it is our responsibility to point that desire in the proper direction. A man that has a wife should focus his sexual desire and energy on that wife and the wife should do the same for the husband. Those that are single must pray for God to help them to discipline and restrain this desire until God gives them a companion. Remember what Paul said! He said that it is better to be unmarried because the unmarried have no obligations except to the Lord, but it is also better to marry than to burn with desire (see 1 Corinthians 7:7-10).

- **Uncleanness** – The Greek word here means "impurity" and could be applied both physically and morally. It seems that we have forgotten the command to *"be ye holy even as I am holy"* (1 Peter 1:16) in a culture where anything and everything is acceptable. Peter would also say a verse before the one just mentioned: *"But as He which hath called you is holy, so be ye holy in all manner of conversation"* (1 Peter 1:15). Holiness may seem like a mark that is so far above what we are able to obtain but we must still strive for this mark daily! Thanks be to God that His blood is more than enough to perfect us and make us holy in our spirit man. Hebrews 10:14 says *"For by one offering he hath perfected forever them that are sanctified."* God has done His part in making us holy and righteous through the offering of His own son and the blood that was shed at Calvary. Now, we must do our part to live a life that is morally and physically clean to the best of our ability! Let us clean up our married lives! Let us clean up our business and financial dealings! Let us clean up our thought processes and the things that we meditate on! Let us clean up the dirty places of our hearts that still want to hide things like jealousy, pride, prejudice, hatred and anger! And how do we do that? Paul was speaking to husbands about loving their wives when he explained to us exactly what Christ has done for His church: *"Christ also loved the church, and gave himself for it; 26 That he might sanctify and cleanse it*

19

with the washing of water by the word" Ephesians 5:25b, 26.

- *Inordinate Affection* – This word speaks of a "passion" that would cause the person to suffer. We see much of this in our world today although we do not recognize it for what it is. We have athletes that are so hungry or passionate about winning and being successful that they will even take drugs that damage the body. We have men and women that are so passionate about the person they are involved with (many times, not even married to) that they do harm to themselves or allow the other person to harm them mentally, emotionally, and sometimes even physically. I do want to note that if you are married, you should be willing to endure hardship, sacrifice personal pleasure at times and compromise your desires to make the marriage work. However, true love never includes abuse. Sacrificial love does not mean that one must lie down and be a doormat or a punching bag. A man or woman that is willing to endure severe abuse or entertain the thought of self-harm or suicide because of their "deep love" for another is guilty of inordinate affection. Another area that we often do not recognize inordinate affection is with our children. While our children deserve and need our unconditional love and support, our "passion" for them should never be so deep that we neglect our responsibility as a spouse. Our love for our children and their contentment should never override our love and commitment to God. In many homes, the commandment is broken: "*Thou shalt have no other gods before me*" (Exodus 20:3) when it comes to our spouse or children. If ever our spouse or children become gods to us, this is inordinate affection. The most noticeable area is materialism: a love and desire for possessions, cars, boats, houses, land, etc. Let us consider what Jesus said in Matthew 6:24 "*No man can serve two masters: for either he will hate the one, and love the other; or else he will hold to the one, and despise the other. Ye cannot serve God and mammon.*" Mammon is defined as "wealth." While wealth and money are not sinful in themselves, we commit a great sin when they become a god to us! Money and wealth can be of great benefit for a Believer that wants to support the work of God and help the hurting but may we never forget what Paul wroteto Timothy: "*For the love of money is the root of all evil: which while some coveted after, they have erred from the faith, and pierced themselves through with many sorrows*" 1 Timothy 6:10.

- *Evil Concupiscence* – This speaks of an "ungodly longing" especially for that which is forbidden. It is lust or worthless desire for things that are not acceptable. Many of these areas border each other closely, but things such as homosexuality, pedophilia, bestiality and incest would all fall into this category. A longing for things that should not

21

be desired at all. The drug and addiction epidemic of this generation would also fall into this category. It is not natural, nor should it be acceptable for a man to want to inject, inhale or smoke the things that they are putting into their bodies today.

• *Covetousness, which is idolatry* – The word here for "covetousness" means greed. Greed is at the root of covetousness, and Paul goes on to say that it is idolatry. God made it plain when handing down the law to Moses how He felt about covetousness. Exodus 20:17 records it like this: *"Thou shalt not covet thy neighbour's house, thou shalt not covet thy neighbour's wife, nor his manservant, nor his maidservant, nor his ox, nor his ass, nor any thing that is thy neighbour's."* But how does this relate to idolatry? Simply put, idolatry is taking an object or an image and worshipping that. Without realizing it, that is exactly what we do when we covet or desire what belongs to someone else, we are giving worship to that item. We must never forget that God put the beautiful, pleasant and even costly things here on earth for us to enjoy, not to long after. The opposite of covetousness is contentment. If we would learn the discipline of contentment, we would not carry the baggage of debt, the baggage of unhappiness, nor the baggage of jealousy. Paul had learned this mindset through his many afflictions and trials. This is what he says in his letter to the Philippians

"11 Not that I speak in respect of want: for I have learned, in whatsoever state I am, therewith to be content. 12 I know both how to be abased, and I know how to abound: every where and in all things I am instructed both to be full and to be hungry, both to abound and to suffer need. 13 I can do all things through Christ which strengtheneth me" Philippians 4:11-13. Let us learn whatever state we are in, whether abased (brought low) or abounding (in excess), full or hungry, our source of strength and substance is Christ and we can do all things through Him.

• *Anger and Wrath* – Anger and wrath go closely together with the major difference being that "anger" is the emotion or the strong feeling of annoyance, displeasure or hostility. Everyone gets angry at some point and it is a natural reaction to a certain extent but we are warned to *"Be ye angry, and sin not: let not the sun go down upon your wrath:"* Ephesians 4:26. Anger is the emotion or the feeling but when it goes unchecked and uncontrolled it will most definitely turn into wrath. Wrath is the action resulting from anger. It is vengeful, it is extreme, and it is forceful. As I write this, it seems to me that we are living in an "angry society." We are angry because someone drove too slowly. We areangry because our food was too cold. We are angry because our children are too loud. We are angry because our spouse is too stubborn. We areangry because the Wi-Fi is too slow. We go to bed

23

angry and we wake up angry. We are angry at the President. We are angry at our boss. We are angry at our neighbors. We are angry at our parents. We are angry, angry, angry! And as a result, we are seeing an increase in wrath. We are seeing senseless violence and murder because we have allowed our anger to go unchecked and uncontrolled.

- *Malice* – The word used here for malice speaks of being wicked or naughty and covers a wide arena of things. It speaks of the inward desire to do evil or to have ill will. Malice is the purposeful intention to cause someone else injury, harm or suffering. This differs from anger and wrath because it does not need anything to happen to create this reaction. It is the result of a deep-seated, inner hostility or meanness. This too is becoming more prevalent in our society as video games, the internet and television have become polluted by scenes of murder, torment, rape, and needless bloodshed. These scenes are imprinted on young, impressionable minds and it warps their ability to think logically. We see the manifestation of malice when a young man will drive hundreds of miles (with plenty of time to reconsider his plans) and shoot innocent people. Let us strive to turn away from anything that is unlike Christ and promotes this sort of ungodly hatred.

- *Blasphemy* – Blasphemy is the insulting or irreverence for God and holy things. The sacredness and holiness of God have always been under attack. In the beginning, His one commandment to abstain from the Tree of Knowledge of Good and Evil was attacked by the serpent. God's peculiar people, The Jewish People have been persecuted for centuries. Even today, books are published and movies are released that criticize, mock and make jest of the things of God. The sad part is that these blasphemies do not come from just the world. Even "religious" people are guilty of disrespecting the House of God and profaning His Holy Law. Paul warned Timothy in 2 Timothy 3:1-5 that the last days would be perilous times. He gave a list characterizing the hearts and condition of men living in those perilous times. In verse two, Paul names "blasphemers" in that list. Although blasphemy is increasing in the days that we are living in and will continue to increase even after the rapture of the Church, God's people must be careful to maintain the standard of holiness and live a life of reverence for our Creator and all of the things that He declares as sacred.

- *Filthy communication* – The word "communication" speaks first of speech but includes the conduct or behavior of a man. Filthy communication is any speech or conduct that is unclean or unwholesome. Believers have no place in the dirty, deplorable ditches of worldly pleasure and entertainment. 2 Timothy 2:19 says *"Nevertheless the foundation of God standeth sure, having this seal, The Lord knoweth them that are his. And, Let every one that nameth the name of Christ depart from iniquity."* God knows that we belong to Him and as Christians we should bear the name of Christ gladly but also with humility, reverence and trembling, being careful to steer clear of things that are sinful. Being saved by grace does not give us a license to sin; it gives a liberty from sin. As believers, let us watch the things that come out of our mouth and the way that we conduct ourselves. As Paul advised the believers of his day, let us also *"abstain from all appearance of sin"* (1 Thessalonians 5:22), and *"Let no corrupt communication proceed out of your mouth, but that which is good to the use of edifying, that it may minister grace unto the hearers."* (Ephesians 4:29).

- *Lying* – Dishonesty appears to be an easy trait to come by. Lying is, simply put, the declaration of an untrue statement. Television and social media have made this simple to do. So simple, that one must dig for the truth and not settle for what is seen or heard. The quality of integrity and honesty is a rare gem to find even in the world's most prominent positions. "Untruth" seems to be pouring out from every direction but the Child of God ought to strive to do as Jesus instructed: *"But let your communication be, Yea, yea; Nay, nay: for whatsoever is more than these cometh of evil"*

26

(Matthew 5:37). Let your communication be simple, straight forward and a declaration of truth, never mingled with deception or trickery.

We would be shocked at how many believers complain about a defeated, empty Christian experience but engage in one or more of these activities that God has labeled as "accursed." Let us follow Joshua's example. Let us remove, destroy, or mortify the "accursed things" that we might once again (or for the first time) enjoy the victory that God has promised.

At this point, you might be asking: "What does any of this have to do with stretching?" The truth is, these things – the "accursed things" are usually the root of our problems. Many times, God will get the blame for a situation when, in reality, we have areas of our life that are accursed because of disobedience. Shake off these areas of disobedience, align your life with the Instructions of God's Word and watch God begin to stretch you to places of newfound victory! That is exactly what God did for Joshua.

For I Will Give It Into Thine Hand

Chapter 8 begins with a word from the Lord for Joshua: "*And the LORD said unto Joshua, Fear not, neither be thou dismayed: take all the people of war with thee, and arise, go up to Ai: see, I have given into thy hand the king of Ai, and his people, and his city, and his land: 2 And thou shalt do to Ai and her king as thou didst unto Jericho and her king: only the spoil thereof, and the cattle thereof, shall ye take for a prey unto yourselves: lay thee an ambush for the city behind it"* (Joshua 8:1,2). Joshua chooses thirty thousand mighty men and sends them out with an instruction to *"lie in wait"* until Joshua and the others draw them out of the city. Just as hoped for, the King of Ai sees them, he and all the inhabitants of Ai go out to pursue them into the wilderness. At this point, God speaks to Joshua again: *"And the LORD said unto Joshua, **Stretch** out the spear that is in thy hand toward Ai; **for I will give it into thine hand.** And Joshua **stretched** out the spear that he had in his hand toward the city"* (Joshua 8:18). After we have removed the "accursed things" from our lives and shaken off fear, we can expect God to begin stretching us! He tells Joshua to stretch out his spear toward Ai, the very village that had defeated Israel. I would like to say to you: God wants to give you victory in the very areas that have troubled you! Whether you have struggled with addiction, a bad temper, a torn marriage, a sick body, a tattered financial life, or a host of other things, stretch out your hand! Expect God to manifest Himself in that area and bring Himself glory in that same area!

If God has promised you victory and possession, stretch your hand in faith! Look at what happens as Joshua stretches his spear toward Ai: *"And the ambush arose quickly out of their place, and they ran as soon as he had stretched out his hand: and they entered into the city, and took it, and hasted and set the city on fire. 20 And when the men of Ai looked behind them, they saw, and, behold, the smoke of the city ascended up to heaven, and they had no power to flee this way or that way: and the people that fled to the wilderness turned back upon the pursuers. 21 And when Joshua and all*

Israel saw that the ambush had taken the city, and that the smoke of the city ascended, then they turned again, and slew the men of Ai. 22 And the other issued out of the city against them; so they were in the midst of Israel, some on this side, and some on that side: and they smote them, so that they let none of them remain or escape. 23 And the king of Ai they took alive, and brought him to Joshua" Joshua 8:19-23. God brought complete victory and possession of the city of Ai to Joshua and the Israelites because Joshua was willing to stretch! And he kept stretching! Verse 26 tells us *"For Joshua drew not his hand back, wherewith he stretched out the spear, until he had utterly destroyed all the inhabitants of Ai."* Keep believing! Keep praying! Keep obeying! Keep stretching until you see full victory in your life! Do not let even one single area of your life slip away through unbelief or disobedience. The promises in His Word belong to you! Do not let anything keep you from fully having every one of them! As a matter of fact, let's look at some promises that we can personally claim in the Word of God!

1. *Salvation* – Jesus was talking about the Salvation experience when He spoke to Nicodemus in John 3:3 *"Verily, verily, I say unto thee, Except a man be born again, he cannot see the kingdom of God."* Nicodemus would follow this statement by asking the question in verse 4: *"How can a man be born when he is old? Can he enter the second time into his mother's womb, and be born?"* It is a difficult concept to grasp with the natural mind to be "born again." Jesus would explain by saying that *"That which is born of the flesh is flesh; and that which is born of the Spirit is spirit"* (see John

29

3:6). The natural birthing process is a physical one and the spiritual birthing process of being "born again" is brought about by the Spirit of God. Jesus said in verse 5: *"Except a man be born of water and of the Spirit, he cannot enter into the kingdom of God."* A man or woman can ONLY come into the Kingdom of God through the washing of the water of the Word of God and by being brought new life through the Spirit of God. Many "Church Goers" are living well beneath the privileges of a child of God because they have never stretched in faith enough to receive this promise. They have allowed the accursed things of this life to keep them back from believing God and being granted new life in the Spirit. And while it is a difficult concept to understand with the natural mind, it is a very real possibility if we will believe and act on the Word of God. Paul brought it down as simply as he could in Romans 10:9, 10: *"9 That if thou shalt confess with thy mouth the Lord Jesus, and shalt believe in thine heart that God hath raised him from the dead, thou shalt be saved. 10 For with the heart man believeth unto righteousness; and with the mouth confession is made unto salvation."* Can you stretch your faith enough to believe with your heart and confess with your mouth what the Bible says about Jesus Christ? Certainly, you can! And if you will, you can have the promise of Salvation!

2. *Sanctification* – To many, the word "sanctification" has the feeling of a rigid, dull life in which a believer can't do certain things and must abstain from going to various places. This could not be further from the

picture we see in scripture of the sanctified life. Scripture teaches us that Jesus died not only to save us from our sins but also to sanctify us to Himself. Hebrews 13:12 says *"Wherefore Jesus also, that he might sanctify the people with his own blood, suffered without the gate."* His sacrificial death paid the penalty for our sins and sets us free from the burden of judgment resulting from those sins. His death also purchased us from the one that wanted to destroy our souls. Now we belong personally and completely to God through sanctification. We are His prized possession. *"19 What? know ye not that your body is the temple of the Holy Ghost which is in you, which ye have of God, and ye are not your own? 20 For ye are bought with a price: therefore glorify God in your body, and in your spirit, which are God's"* (1 Corinthians 6:19, 20). Once we realize that we can live in this sacred place of sanctification and that we can be used of God in a special, peculiar way, our lifestyle begins to change. Salvation started a work in the heart but through Sanctification, all areas of our lives are affected. Our speech, our work ethic, our business dealings, our attire, our hobbies, our attitudes, our interests and our relationships will all begin to reflect this newly discovered identity in Christ. Stretch your faith to believe this wonderful promise of God and allow the consecrating work of sanctification to have its way in your mind and life!

3. *Healing and Good Health* – A sad misconception, even among God's people, is that sickness is from God. Some feel like they must endure sickness "to

learn a lesson" or "to pray more" or because they are being punished for something. We must understand that "every good gift and every perfect gift is from above, and cometh down from the Father of lights" (James 1:17). If it isn't good and it isn't perfect, it did not come from God. God may allow something (as He did with Job), but He is never the source of the terrible things that Satan tries to hurl at mankind. Jesus also made it plain that He came that we might have life and have it abundantly but that the thief (the devil) came with the intention of stealing, killing and destroying (John 10:10). Christ's death on the Cross is more than a cure for sin. It is the remedy for sickness, pain and disease. The Prophet Isaiah, speaking of Christ, centuries before He would come, said this about His suffering and death: *"3 He is despised and rejected of men; a man of sorrows, and acquainted with grief: and we hid as it were our faces from Him; He was despised, and we esteemed Him not. 4 Surely He hath borne our griefs, and carried our sorrows: yet we did esteem Him stricken, smitten of God, and afflicted. 5 But He was wounded for our transgressions, He was bruised for our iniquities: the chastisement of our peace was upon Him, and **with His stripes we are healed**"* (Isaiah 53:3-5). When they whipped our blessed savior, ripping and tearing the flesh on His back, those stripes were put there for our healing: physically, mentally and spiritually. The scriptures are filled with stories and examples of God's healing power. He brought sight to the blind. He gave strength to crippled legs. He opened ears that were stopped. He dried up the flowing of blood. He even called the dead back to life. Is anything too hard for God? For a redeemed person, sickness cannot hold us back. This does not mean that we won't get sick and suffer pain and affliction like any other person. It does mean that we can be miraculously, divinely healed while here on the earth. And in cases where healing does not manifest here, God gives sufficient grace to make it through each trial and then complete healing when this life is over. Until then, we ought to stretch and believe God for every promise in the Book, including John's desire for the Church, to *"prosper and be in health, evenas thy soul prospereth"* (1 John 1:2).

4. **Baptism in the Holy Spirit** – Jesus told His disciples to *"wait for the promise of the Father, which, saith He, ye have heard of Me. 5 For John truly baptized with water; but ye shall be baptized with the Holy Ghost not many days hence"* (Acts 1:4,5). This "Promise of the Father" was the supernatural "Baptism of the Holy Ghost." Tragically, the Holy Ghost Baptism is written off by some as an experience that no longer occurs. But Peter preached in Acts 2:39 *"For the promise is unto you, and to your children, and to all that are afar off, even as many as the Lord our God shall call."* God, speaking through the Prophet Joel, declared *"I will pour out My Spirit upon all flesh; and your sons and your daughters shall prophesy, your old men shall dream dreams, your young men shall see visions:"* (Joel 2:28). God gave the initial outpouring in Acts, Chapter 2 to those disciples that obediently went and tarried at Jerusalem until the promise came but it did not stop

33

there. Several other groups are recorded in scripture as receiving this experience after the Day of Pentecost (Acts 4:31, Acts 8:14-17, Acts 10:44-46, Acts 19:1-6). Paul's letter to the Corinthians lets us know that the Holy Ghost was still moving and ministering years later in the Corinthian Church (1 Corinthians, Chapters 12 & 14). The evidence of The Holy Ghost Baptism experience is "speaking in other tongues" but don't be misled into thinking that is all that it consists of. Jesus gave us the real purpose for the Holy Ghost Baptism in Acts 1:8 *"But **ye shall receive power**, after that the Holy Ghost is come upon you: and **ye shall be witnesses** unto me both in Jerusalem, and in all Judaea, and in Samaria, and unto the uttermost part of the earth."* The Holy Ghost Baptism is about accepting the fullness of the power of God – not to manifest some odd behavior or to merely speak in an unlearned language – but that we might be effective witnesses for Jesus where we are and everywhere that we go. This Holy Ghost Baptism will make a difference on your job. It will affect your marriage. It will influence your children. It will change the atmosphere in your church. This Holy Ghost Power transformed Peter from a cowardly backslider into a mighty man of God willing to step out and even die for his faith. This Holy Ghost Power will cause the Gifts of the Spirit to operate in your worship experience. It will cause the Fruit of the Spirit to flourish and thrive in your everyday life. The Holy Ghost is a teacher, a comforter, a companion and a guide (John 14:26, John 15:26). If you are barely getting by in your Christian experience, stretch your faith and believe God for this beautiful experience of the Holy Ghost Baptism! Stretch out your hand in obedience (Acts 5:32), "wait for the promise" and be endued with this life-changing power!

5. *Financial Security* – Financial security is NOT about having a lot of money. From my observation, more money has never made a person more secure. Financial security IS about being content with the things that you have (Hebrews 13:5, Philippians 4:11, 12) and trusting God for the things that you need (Matthew 6:25-32). In Matthew 6, Jesus gave us two examples of how our Heavenly Father is able to take care of us. First, He talked about the *"fowls of the air"* (Matthew 6:26). They do not worry about sowing seed, reaping harvests or storing up in barns. Rather, they are fed and cared for by the Father. Then Jesus asked the question: *"Are ye not much better than they?"* Second, He spoke of the *"lilies of the field"* (Matthew 6:28). He noted how they are not able to toil or to spin material to make their raiment, but they are clothed with more splendor than the great King Solomon. God, who takes care of all His Creation, promises to take good care of us but we let so small a thing as money cause us so much heartache and trouble. Paul even warned his young apprentice, Timothy *"For the love of money is the root of all evil: which while some coveted after, they have erred from the faith, and pierced themselves through with many sorrows"* (1 Timothy 6:10).

God asks so little of us in the realm of finances, yet we make it so difficult. First, He asks us to honor Him with our tithes and offerings (Malachi 3:10). If we are faithful in that, He declares that He will do several things on our behalf. 1. He will open the windows of heaven and pour out such a blessing that we do not have room to receive it all (Malachi 3:10). 2. He will rebuke the devourer for our sakes. He will not allow the devil or any of his hateful plans to succeed in destroying the fruit of our labors (Malachi 3:11) 3. Others would recognize the Blessings of God on your life as the nations call you blessed and see you as a delightsome land (Malachi 3:12). Secondly, He asks us to give happily and not begrudgingly. 2 Corinthians 9:7 *"Every man according as he purposeth in his heart, so let him give; not grudgingly, or of necessity: for God loveth a cheerful giver."* Thirdly, He instructs us to give simply and not as a spectacle for others to see us (Matthew 6:1-4). Our giving to God and our giving to those in need is a private, quiet act of worship and does not need to be paraded in front of others. If we do it in secret, God is honored and will reward us openly. Again, in the realm of finances, God asks very little of us, but offers benefits far above what we deserve. Concerning our finances, let us stretch past our selfish wants and desire and *"seek first the Kingdom of God, and His righteousness"* and we can experience true financial security as He has promised *"all these things shall be added unto you"* (Matthew 6:33).

6. *Mental Clarity* – Mental health is so important yet often ignored in Christian circles. Could this be the reason why so many of our members are heavily medicated? Could this be the reason why even our Pastors are coming under bondage to things like drugs, alcohol or sexual addiction? Is it possible that people we thought were "good Christians" are resorting to the dreadful end of suicide because we refuse to deal with the taboo issues concerning mental health and clarity? Could it be that we spend so much of our time preaching a standard of holiness that deals only with our physical appearance, our Church attendance, financial giving and what is expected of us by our families, the Church, and the world that we disregard the realm of the mind? I'm glad that God in His Word has not overlooked the mental state of man. Rather, He has given us plenty of instruction and even a promise that He will keep us in perfect peace if our minds are stayed on Him (see Isaiah 26:3)! Paul gives us the illustration of the Helmet of Salvation as being part of our spiritual armor (Ephesian 6:17). This relates to us the fact that Salvation is not just a "heart" work. Salvation covers the mind as well! In 1 Thessalonians 5:8 Paul encourages believers to put on for a *"helmet, the hope of salvation."* The very fact that we are saved, and the hope of God's glorious salvation will do a work in the mental realm of the believer.

Be warned, it will not happen overnight. One minister said, "You can't keep a bird from flying over your head, but you sure can keep him from building a nest in your hair!" The devil is a master of deception. He will shoot fiery darts right into your mind! Thoughts of ugliness, criticism, negativity, racism, depression, hatred, unforgiveness, perversion, death and suicide can all be traced right back to the enemy of our soul. What do we do when an ungodly, unbiblical thought pops into our mind? We recognize it for the bad seed that it is and pluck it out. We immediately grab for that helmet of salvation, thanking God that we are saved from every trick and tactic of the devil and we refuse to give him ANY room in our minds (see Ephesians 4:27). We submit ourselves (including our minds) to the Lord and ask Him to renew and transform our mind and our thinking (Romans 12:2, Ephesians 4:23)

Monitoring what we meditate on is half the battle. If you meditate on things that make you mad, anger is going to control your mind. If you focus on the negative things that people have done to you, unforgiveness is going to cloud your mind. If you think on dirty and perverted things, lust and immorality is going to contaminate your mind like poison. The psalmist gave the qualities of the "Blessed Man" in Psalm 1. He does not surround himself with the ungodly and scornful. Verse 2 tells us that he also controls what he meditates on: *"His delight is in the law of the LORD; and in His law doth he meditate day and night."* Paul gives us a check list of things to "think on" in Philippians 4:8. *"Finally, brethren, whatsoever*

22.

*things are **true**, whatsoever things are **honest**, whatsoever things are **just**, whatsoever things are **pure**, whatsoever things are **lovely**, whatsoever things are **of good report**; if there be any **virtue**, and if there be any **praise**, think on these things.*" It takes intensive effort, but if we will use this one verse to examine every thought, we will reap amazing benefits in the realm of our mental health. If a thought is true, honest, just, pure, lovely, of a good report, contains virtue and praise, THINK ON THESE things! However, if a thought does not meet the requirements of this verse, discard that thought and think about something else that does.

Mental illness and disease are very real, and many people require medical, professional help and medication. We will not in any way discount or discredit that. However, for the vast multitudes of believers and unbelievers alike, a simple adjustment in the things that we think about will bring about tremendous change in our mental state, our attitude and our perspective on life. Are you willing to stretch past the lowly and base thoughts of this world and fix your mind on Jesus to obtain that peace of mind that is promised to you? Keep stretching your mind toward the heights of God's Word and He will give you a peace of mind that surpasses human understanding (see Philippians 4:7).

7. *Household Salvation* – Every Christian knows the sting of living the Christian life while having family members that are lost and have not yet come to the saving knowledge of Jesus Christ. Do not settle for

thinking that it will always be this way! Do not settle for letting the devil have your children and your companion, your parents or even your siblings, nieces, nephews or grandchildren! This faith that we are so graciously a part of is not good enough for one or two, it is good for the whole family, for the whole house! For the believing wife with the heathen husband (and vice versa), God gives you a promise: *"For the unbelieving husband is sanctified by the wife, and the unbelieving wife is sanctified by the husband:"* This promise is also good for your children that don't know the Lord: *"else were your children unclean; but now are they holy"* (see 1 Corinthians 7:14). We are quick to throw away or cut off communication with those family members that are hard to love or disrespect the things that we believe and know about God. But your sanctified life, your communication of the Gospel and your outpouring of the Love of God is just what they need! Paul would ask these husbands and wives just a few verses down in verse 16: *"For what knowest thou, O wife, whether thou shalt save thy husband? or how knowest thou, O man, whether thou shalt save thy wife?"*

1 Samuel 25 tells us the story of a beautiful, understanding woman by the name of Abigail that was married to a foolish, obstinate, wicked man by the name of Nabal. Nabal had gotten himself in a situation where he was biting off more than he could chew. Instead of speaking respectably to king David and his men, he acted foolishly, and David was ready

to destroy Nabal and all that were with him. This sensible woman Abigail went quickly to David with gifts and pled for mercy. This act of wisdom resulted in Nabal's life being spared from king David. Are you willing to stretch beyond the nonsense of some of your family members? Are you willing to look beyond what they deserve and plead for God's mercy on their lives? That's what this woman did, and the king spared his life.

In his sermon on the day of Pentecost, Peter preached that the gift of the Holy Ghost was not just for us, but it was also for our children: *"For the promise is unto you, and to your children, and to all that are afar off, even as many as the Lord our God shall call"* (Acts 2:39). In Acts 16, we see this "Household Salvation" at work as Paul and Silas and all the other prisoners were miraculously delivered from the jail where they were held captive. The jailor, fearing the consequences he would face, was about to take his life with his own sword. Paul and Silas took this as an opportunity to preach the Gospel and challenged the man to *"Believe on the Lord Jesus Christ, and thou shalt be saved, and thy house"* (Acts 16:31). That same night, that jailor *"was baptized, he and all his, straightway"* (Acts 16:33). Newly converted and freshly baptized, this jailor took these preachers to his house and fed them and *"rejoiced, believing in God with all his house"* (Acts 16:34). The jailor found out what you and I can experience for ourselves: This salvation is good for the whole household! Do not settle for letting your family die lost, never knowing the pleasure of walking with God, living in His Presence and having sweet fellowship with Him. Keep stretching your faith, your patience and your love for your family and declare as Joshua did: *"as for me and my house, we will serve the LORD"* (Joshua 24:15).

All these things and so much more belong to you if you are a child of God! Don't let the devil trick you out of these blessings. Don't let your flesh and temporary pleasure cheat you out of the full abundant life that God promised. Keep stretching even when it's difficult, even when you see no immediate results. Keep stretching even when others may ridicule you. Keep stretching even when you seem to be standing alone! The promises of God belong to you if you can SURVIVE THE STRETCHING!

CHAPTER 3
The Bottom of the Barrel

I f you have never been at the bottom of the barrel, this chapter may not mean as much to you. However, for countless multitudes of people spanning the globe, the bottom of the barrel is a reality.Living from paycheck to paycheck is the only life thatsome people know. If you are among the few that areprivileged to have never known scarcity, thank God foryour blessings! For the rest of us, we know the uncertainty of the bottom of the barrel and the struggle of SURVIVING THE STRETCHING!

Sometimes, amid a trial or a hardship, it can feel like God is stretching you. At other times, God will stretch the resources around you. This is what we find in 1 Kings 17. Elijah has been down at the brook Cherith, hiding from the heathen king, Ahab and his wicked wife, Jezebel. But it isn't Elijah that is surviving the stretching. He is well taken care of. He gets to drink from the cool, clear waters of the brook Cherith. God is sending him bread and flesh every morning and every evening by way of ravens (see 1 Kings 17:4-6). Things begin to change course in verse 7 as *"the brook dried up, because there had been no rain in the land."* God speaks to Elijah that it is time to get up and go to Zarephath because Hehad *"commanded a widow woman there to sustain"* Elijah (1Kings 17:9).

Obedient to the Word of the Lord, Elijah gets up and heads to Zarephath. I am not sure what Elijah was expecting but he does not find what I would have expected. I would have expected a wealthy widow. I would have expected a woman with the means to support herself as well as company. Elijah finds the widow at the gate of the city, gathering sticks. He calls to her and says, *"Fetch me, I pray thee, a little water in a vessel, that I may drink"* (1 Kings 17:10). The widow woman turns to head back home to get it when Elijah calls to her a second time with another request: *"Bring me, I pray thee, a morsel of bread in thine hand"* (1 Kings 17:11).

Verse 12 is where the story turns, and we see the real situation and the widow's plight. She was fine with fixing him a glass of water, but a slice of bread was not a possibility in her home at this point. She answers Elijah *"As the Lord thy God liveth, I have not a cake, but an handful of meal in a barrel, and a little oil in a cruse: and behold, I am gathering two sticks, that I may go in and dress it for me and my son, that we may eat it and die."* This woman cannot afford to feed another person. Why would God send Elijah to a place with few resources and an even bleaker hope? This woman wasn't ready for visitors, she was ready to die. Her husband's death coupled with a lack of rain and resources in the land created for this woman the perfect disaster. Perhaps God sent Elijah to this woman's address because He does His best work when our backs are against the wall. The perfect disaster is fertile ground for a miracle if a person is obedient to God's Word and willing to follow the Spirit's prompting.

Poverty Today

I know it is hard to comprehend, but for the People of God, there are innumerable opportunities to see God work in the same way today as He did for Elijah and the widow woman. Poverty surrounds us on every side and God can do the miraculous and provide for His people supernaturally if we are daring enough to believe Him and be obedient to His Word!

Is it possible that there are folks near despair because of a lack of food or resources? Even in a society where there are food banks and soup kitchens in every city? Could a person be at rock bottom with multiple handouts and assistance programs available? Is it possible for a person to be so hopeless and be ready to die? In America? In a land blessed beyond measure? The answer is YES!

At the time of this writing, I have been involved in feeding the hungry for more than ten years. I have seen my fair share of the greedy, the lazy and the self-serving. I have seen those that would not work in a pie factory tasting cherries as the old saying goes. I have seen many starving to death because they would rather spend their last dime on drugs, alcohol, sex or lottery tickets. I have encountered people that would wait in line for hours to receive a box of food while their cupboards were lined and filled. But for every story like that, I have seen real people struggling to make ends meet. For every greedy person, for every lazy person, for every person seeking a handout when they do not need it, there is an elderly person that has worked his entire life to retire with more bills than the amount of their pension. There are disabled individuals (many crippled while serving and protecting our nation) that must decide between groceries and necessary medications; between canned goods and a pack of toilet paper; between buying meat for the freezer and saving up to pay an upcoming tax or insurance bill. There are grandparents, some stretching into their 70's raising grandchildren that they cannot afford to feed. But for every one of these heart-breaking stories, I have seen God show Himself faithful, especially to His children!

Fear Not!

We can join Elijah in his message to the widow woman: *"Fear Not!"* (See 1 Kings 17:13). For those struggling with poverty and scarcity, it is easy to be overwhelmed with a sense of fear. Where is the next meal coming from? How are the bills going to be paid? Is this where it all ends?

I recall a time when I recognized this sense of fear overtaking an individual. I had received a call from a lady in desperate need of help. "Anything will help!" I remember her saying after describing her dilemma to me. She was the wife of a disabled husband and the primary breadwinner in the home. As if their situation was not tight enough, she had recently assumed custody of two grandchildren to keep them out of foster care. This is a reality for many families today! As I pulled up to the address that she had given me, I saw the home's dilapidated condition and I knew that her situation was just as bad as she had told me, if not worse!

As I walked into the home, I was greeted and welcomed as if I was part of the family although this family had never met me before. The grandchildren were sitting at a rickety table eating a bowl of noodles. They were so excited to see that small box of food come into the house. You would have thought that I had brought presents and toys. The grandmother was grateful, but I could see the sadness on her face and the fear in her eyes. This small box of food and puny check were both small compared to the weight and burden that sat on her shoulders.

Let us be sure to preach it and to proclaim it even in the most tragic of circumstances: Fear Not! As Christians, we have the answers to the problems of poverty and we have the cure for the spirit of fear, even today! God is faithful and will make a way for His people just as He has promised! *"I have been young, and now am old; yet have I not seen the righteous forsaken, nor Hisseed begging bread"* Psalm 37:25.

Make Me A Little Cake First

This may seem like a strange place to speak about giving but it is an important key in terms of finances, resources, and even times of need. The tithe is more than a percentage of your income. Many of us give to God as we would pay a bill. We grudgingly calculate ten percent and angrily throw it in the offering plate (if we do it at all). In other cases, we may give the tithe as an investment in a corporation. Because we give, we are entitled to a voice, a vote or having our way in certain areas. We complain about what THEY are doing with our money. We criticize leadership and Church functions and ministries and if we can at all justify ourselves, we will even withhold our giving until THEY start making better decisions. Can I warn you today that our giving has nothing to do with the THEY that may manage it? Giving is a covenant agreement between you and the Giver of all good things!

He blesses us with 100% of ALL that we own. Vehicles, homes, jobs, income, possessions are all a gift from God. "Well," you may say, "I WORKED for that!" I would respond to you with a few questions: "Who gave you the ability to work? Who put strength in your body to perform the tasks that your employer demands? Who gives you the mental capacity to carry out simple functions, and the complex instructions, that you have to follow daily?" None of us are self-made. We have made accomplishments and obtained what we own because of God's grace and His goodness. Out of that 100% that God has given us; He lays out the pattern for bringing a tenth (where we get the word tithe) to come in His storehouse. When you give into your local storehouse, release it. Don't criticize, don't begrudge, don't complain. Smile! Understand that you have done your part and that God is going to do His part in this covenant agreement. This is why Paul wrote in 2 Corinthians 9:7 *"Every man according as he purposeth in his heart, so let him give; not grudgingly, or of necessity: for God loveth a cheerful giver."* God loves a cheerful giver because they understand the concept of giving. They give it in faith and are happy about sowing into the Kingdom of God! Let me tell you, Friend, you will never outgive God! If you shovel it to Him, He will turn around and backhoe it to you!

Elijah tells the woman in verse 13: *"go and do as thou hast said: **but make me thereof a little cake first**, and bring it unto me, and after make for thee and for thy son."* This is a big request for a woman with so little resources; a woman who is ready to make her last meal and wait on death. Something tells me that Elijah understood the concept of giving to God FIRST. Elijah tells her to go and make the cake as she had planned. Instead of her and her son dividing, eating the cake and dying, he tells her to make for him a *"little cake first"* and bring it to him. After she has done this, THEN she could make some for her and her son. With this instruction, as with every instruction from God, there is a promise. Verse 14 says *"For thus saith the LORD God of Israel, The barrel of meal shall not waste, neither shall the cruse of oil fail, until the day that the LORD sendeth rain upon the earth."* Notice that

God did not promise her a whole barrel of meal or a truckload of oil if she was obedient but what He did promise was that He would STRETCH what she had until the rain returned!

How many times have we missed the blessings of God because they weren't huge, massive blessings? How many times has He stretched our $20 bill and we didn't even recognize it because it was not a $200 check? I'm not convinced that if you send your favorite Televangelist your last dollar that God is going to bless you 30, 60 or 100-fold. I am convinced of the principles of God's Word and that if you consistently and faithfully support the work of God and do it cheerfully, out of love and faith, God will stretch what you have! He will make your clothes last longer! He will cause your vehicle to go further! He will cause your income to cover more of your outgoing than you expected! He promised this widow woman, that because of her obedience, He would cause meal to be in the barrel and oil in the vessel every time that she needed it.

The Bottom of the Barrel

There is a blessing in being at the bottom of the barrel. It was during this time that she saw the supernatural power of God in providing for His children. Can you see her day after day? Stretching to scrape the meal from the bottom of the barrel? Can you imagine in the evening as she stretched and pulled up her last full cup of meal, she wondered: "What about tomorrow?" And every morning, she would stretch again to get another full cup of meal. It was at the bottom of the barrel that she saw how faithful God was to her and her home.

Maybe you are at the bottom of the barrel. You have come close to giving up, throwing in the towel. You see what looks like the end with no hope of anything coming in. Perhaps you have lost your home. They came and picked up your car because you couldn't keep up with the payments. Your utilities are close to being turned off. What do you do? You wait on God! He likes to work when nothing else will. He wants you and I to realize that all the luxuries that make us happy and comfortable are not necessities. He wants us to realize that the only thing that we need is more of Him! Keep stretching! Keep scratching the bottom of the barrel! God is faithful and will supply what you NEED when you NEED it!

It Won't Always Be Like This

God had made a promise to the widow woman through the prophet Elijah. 1 Kings 17:14 says *"For thus saith the LORD God of Israel, The barrel of meal shall not waste, neither shall the cruse of oil fail, until the day that the LORD sendeth rain upon the earth."* He did not promise her excess and abundance, but He did promise that He would see her through this famine and this dreaded season in her life. The barrel of meal and the cruse of oil would last until the Lord sent rain again.

The woman responded in obedience because of her faith. Verse 15 tells us *"And she went and did according to*

51

the saying of Elijah: and she, and he, and her house, did eat many days." We do not know exactly how many days, but we know that for many days, she stretched, and she obeyed. God stretched and He provided. Day after day she saw the miraculous while living off barely anything. And day by day God's Word was fulfilled to her. Verse 16 says *"And the barrel of meal wasted not, neither did the cruse of oil fail, according to the word of the LORD, which he spake by Elijah."*

You may be going through a drought, a dry season in your life. Your income is minimal. Your resources are scarce. Others look down on you because of how you barely make it by. Your paychecks run short while your bills continue to come in. Be faithful to God. Trust Him and obey His Word to the best of your ability. And wait. Stretch and wait. Wait and stretch. Things will not always be like this. The seeds that you have sown will produce. The prayers that you have prayed will be answered. The rain will come again. The famine will end. You just have to keep stretching! And if you do, *"…in due season we shall reap, if we faint not"* (Galatians 6:9).

CHAPTER 4
If I May Touch But His Clothes

Have you ever felt unclean? Unaccepted? Not good enough? Sometimes these feelings can come from some mistake we have made. Maybe we got ensnared in some sin that got exposed or even a private sin that the devil is repeatedly condemning us about. Maybe we have some disability or ailment that keeps us from being all that we would like to be. The Gospels introduce us to a woman that knew this feeling of being a societal outcast and has been rejected on many levels. Three out of the four Gospel writers record her story but for the sake of this Chapter, we will see her story from Mark's point of view. If we pay close attention, we will find that God can take anybody, no matter how low they may be and pick them up and give them a fresh start IF they can SURVIVE THE STRETCHING!

The Woman's Issue

Her story starts in Mark, Chapter 5 and Verse 25. She is simply introduced as *"a certain women, which had an issue of blood twelve years."* More than likely her issue was not as horrible as the consequences of having this issue. The probable cause of her bleeding could have been one out of two things: hemorrhoids or menstruation; with the latter more likely the cause. Both causes were normal issues, so her issue was not her issue, so to speak. The real problem was the time frame for which she had endured this problem coupled with the fact that according to The Law of Moses, she was deemed "unclean" until she could be free of her bleeding for 7 consecutive days.

This issue affected every area of this poor woman's life: socially, religiously and even domestically. The Law of Moses spelled out all the things she could NOT do during the time of her blood flow. Leviticus 15:19-30 laid out the many regulations placed on a woman and how she was labeled "unclean" during this already distressing time.

"19 And if a woman have an issue, and her issue in her flesh be blood, she shall be put apart seven days: and whosoever toucheth her shall be unclean until the even. 20 And every thing that she lieth upon in her separation shall be unclean: every thing also that she sitteth upon shall be unclean." The woman's issue of blood automatically required that she be separated from everyone for seven days. Anyone that touched her during this time was also seen as "unclean" until the evening of that day. Everything that she laid on and sat on was perceived as "unclean." Imagine the humiliation and stigma placed on a woman during these seven days. Now imagine twelve long years of this.

"*21 And whosoever toucheth her bed shall wash his clothes, and bathe himself in water, and be unclean until the even. 22 And whosoever toucheth any thing that she sat upon shall wash his clothes, and bathe himself in water, and be unclean until the even. 23 And if it be on her bed, or on any thing whereon she sitteth, when he toucheth it, he shall be unclean until the even.*" The woman was affected socially as the people in her life were unable to visit and fellowship with her as before. They could not touch her bed or anything that she sat on. If they did, they would have to wash in water and still be deemed as unclean until the evening of that day. Again, as if seven days of this type of isolation was not bad enough, imagine dealing with this type of isolation for twelve years.

"*24 And if any man lie with her at all, and her flowers be upon him, he shall be unclean seven days; and all the bed whereon he lieth shall be unclean. 25 And if a woman have an issue of her blood many days out of the time of her separation, or if it run beyond the time of her separation; all the days of the issue of her uncleanness shall be as the days of her separation: she shall be unclean.*" This spoke of how the woman's domestic and relational life was altered because of this issue. All intimacy with her husband was forbidden unless he be labeled unclean as well for seven days. Seven days may not seem like that long to some but pay attention to what it also says in Verse 25. If she had her issue of blood many days during the time of separation or if it lasted longer than the allotted seven days, the time of her separation was extended. Imagine the strain that this would put on any healthy marriage and especially for twelve exasperating years.

"26 Every bed whereon she lieth all the days of her issue shall be unto her as the bed of her separation: and whatsoever she sitteth upon shall be unclean, as the uncleanness of her separation. 27 And whosoever toucheth those things shall be unclean, and shall wash his clothes, and bathe himself in water, and be unclean until the even. 28 But if she be cleansed of her issue, then she shall number to herself seven days, and after that she shall be clean. 29 And on the eighth day she shalltake unto her two turtles, or two young pigeons, and bring them unto the priest, to the door of the tabernacle of the congregation. 30 And the priest shall offer the one for a sin offering, and the other for a burnt offering; and the priest shall make an atonement for her before the LORD for the issue of her uncleanness." Her uncleanness even affected her religious life. It was unacceptable for her to be involved in the synagogue in any way during the time of her separation. She had to wait seven days after the bleedingstopped and then on the eighth day, she was required tobring a special offering to atone for her "uncleanness" (even though this was a normal issue for women to have). Imagine being disengaged from corporate worship and fellowship with other believers for twelve years! My, what this woman went through!

Her issue is a lot like ours except we (in most cases) do not have a written standard against us regulating our life and making us unacceptable. Whatever issue we may be facing, it normally does not affect just one area of our life, but many and sometimes all. Her issue was anormal act of the body that she just could not seem to getunder control or find a remedy for. She even tried many physicians!

She Only Grew Worse

Mark said in the 26th verse that *"she had suffered many things of many physicians, and spent all that she had, and was nothing bettered, but rather grew worse."* This woman spent much of that twelve years going from doctor to doctor, suffering many things. We do not know what kind of treatments, medications or even experimental practices that this woman had to endure but it was not good, and it did her no good. She went through all of this, and instead of getting better, she only grew worse! Picture the despair and oppression she must have felt. She was going through this while under the scrutinizing eye of the community. Spending all that she had with no positive results.

You may be reading this and know exactly how she feels. You have tried everything. You have read self-help books. You have joined support groups. You have talked to doctors and have been referred to specialists. You may have tried a 3 step, 5 step or even maybe a 10 step program. You have been prayed over, preached to and advised of what someone else thinks you ought to do. And you look back after you have done everything, tried everything and spent everything and you are no better! Actually, you are worse! I want to give you a Word of encouragement! Don't give up there! There is someone in your corner and this pitiful woman found out from someone about this man named Jesus!

When She Had Heard

Mark tells us that someone told this woman about Jesus! Verse 27 says *"When she had heard of Jesus..."* Hearing about Him changed her attitude and it changed the course that she was on. If you are a Christian, I want to challenge you to think a minute about how seriously you take your call to share your faith. Many Christians think they have done well by going to Church once a week (and some do not go that often). We have been deceived into thinking that we have met our obligation by putting some money in the plate, giving to someone in need or supporting a missionary that stirred us emotionally. I want you to recognize that we have not even scratched the surface of carrying out the command that Jesus left with us: *"Go ye into all the world and preach the gospel to every creature"* (Mark 16:15). We may not be able to go into ALL the world, but the entire world could be reached with the Gospel if EVERY believer did their part in telling this good news!

You are surrounded by people that need help. Like the woman in our story, they have tried everything, and nothing is working. If you are in a personal relationship with Jesus, you have the answer. You can tell them from experience what He has done for you and how He can change life for them. Your witness for Him may not move most people but if you keep it to yourself, you will surely hide it from the one that needs to hear it. After all, someone once shared the Gospel with you. You know Him today because someone told you about Him! Go out and tell it. Tell it confidently. Tell it humbly. Tell it without apology. Jesus still saves. He still delivers. He still changes lives. But how will crying, dying humanity ever know if someone doesn't share it?

"13 For whosoever shall call upon the name of the Lord shall be saved. 14 How then shall they call on him in whom they have not believed? and how shall they believe in him of whom they have not heard? and how shall they hear without a preacher? 15 And how shall they preach, except they be sent? as it is written, How beautiful are the feet of them that preach the gospel of peace, and bring glad tidings of good things! 16 But they have not all obeyed the gospel. For Esaias saith, Lord, who hath believed our report? 17 So then faith cometh by hearing, and hearing by the word of God."

Romans 10:13-17

Came In the Press Behind

This woman did not idly listen to some story about a man that claimed to be a Messiah. She listened intently and faith began to bud in her heart. She believed what was told to her about this man! She was so moved that her faith became action. The Bible says in that 27th verse that once she had heard of Jesus, she *"came in the press behind, and touched his garment."* Socially, this was unthinkable. How could this woman risk making all these people "unclean," especially this profound teacher and miracle worker? Her faith rose above custom. It rose above tradition and it rose above "the press." I just want to warn you that "the press" has always been and will always be a hindering force to the move of God. The way

Pastor Kyle Driggers

of Faith is almost always contradictory to what the "crowd" desires and does. It takes someone with a drive to live and thrive to push against the current and go against the grain of tradition and normalcy. Any old dead fish can float with the current.

We have all had things that we dreamt about. Desires to kick some habit or get out of some wicked lifestyle. If you have ever tried to get closer to the Lord, you know what I am about to say is true. The devil will always send by someone to tell you that "you can't do that" or that "you don't have to do that." That's the problem with "the press." The crowd does what is convenient. They do what is easy and their results are minimal to none. Do not allow the crowd to persuade you or dictate to you when it comes to getting your miracle.

Imagine this little woman, told for so many years what she was not allowed to do. Imagine as faith blossoms in her spirit and is activated by her drive to do something! Now, she has to STRETCH! She crawls through the crowd, on her hands and knees. At this point, she has no pride. She desires no glory. She just knows that she is going to touch Him!!! She presses through "the press" and she STRETCHES that feeble hand until she grabs what she intended to get her hands on! Now that is FAITH!

For She Said

The Holy Spirit drops a little nugget here in Verse 28 about faith and receiving what you need from the Lord.

60

"For she said, If I may touch but His clothes, I shall be whole!" Many times, we go to Church, we go to Conventions, we go to Prayer Meetings, but we have not gone to these places with the right mindset. This woman made up her mind before she ever got started that if she could touch even His clothes, she would be made whole! She made a positive confession as to how she was going to receive her miracle.

1. **She had a made-up mind** – She was already convinced of the reality of her miracle. This is faith: the *"substance of things hoped for, the evidence of things not seen"* (Hebrews 11:1). Anyone that ever received anything from the Lord had to first *"believe that He is, and that He is a rewarder of them that diligently seek Him"* (Hebrews 11:6). You cannot be wishy-washy with the things of God. It does not matter how many special services you attend, how long you pray or how many chapters you have read in your Bible if you have not made up your mind to BELIEVE and activate your faith by OBEYING!

2. **She had her confession ready** – Notice that *"she SAID."* Who did she say it to? That is not nearly as important as WHAT she said. Maybe she said it to a neighbor. Maybe she said it to her husband. She may have even said it to the person that witnessed to her about Christ. Or perhaps, she said it to herself! As already stated, WHO you say it to is not nearly as important as WHAT you say. She had a positive confession of faith. *"She SAID If I may touch but His clothes, I shall be whole!"* Do you realize that if you

walk around declaring that you have a miserable life, or how terrible your companion is, or what an awful day you are experiencing, you can expect those things to manifest more and more? But if you will change your confession, it will change the course of your day, your marriage and even your life. Confess the Word of God over every area of your life and BELIEVE what you are confessing.

As I am writing this, my mind goes back to several years ago, when we were holding all-night prayer meetings at the Church we were pastoring. My wife, Tiffany had been saved for quite a few years and had been praying for the Baptism of the Holy Ghost for most of those years. We had been to many Churches, in many services where she would be prayed over and NOTHING would happen. However, during the time that we were having these all-night prayer meetings, On Friday, we would fast all day. We would meet at the Church around 7 pm that evening for our prayer meetings. Fasting was not easy for Tiff and I recall her saying on one of those Fridays "Tonight, I AM GOING to receive the Holy Ghost!" Her stomach was growling, and she was frustrated that she had not eaten anything but right there she made a positive confession concerning that prayer meeting. We prayed for many things that night, including her as we always did but this night was different. Sometime after midnight, the Holy Ghost broke into our little prayer meeting and Tiff was baptized in the Holy Ghost! Do you realize that God still honors His Word and He takes pleasure in His children

STRETCHING their faith beyond what is comfortable, normal, and believing and confessing His Word?

She Was Healed

This woman touched the hem of Jesus' garment and just as she had declared there was a change in her body. Look at what Verse 29 says *"And straightway, the fountain of her blood was dried up; and she felt in her body that she was healed of that plague."* This woman received a miraculous healing immediately after touching His clothes. She had suffered for twelve long years. She had endured isolation. She persevered through unfruitful doctor visits. She had lost all that she had and even grew worse in her body. But when she heard about Jesus, she made up her mind and confessed that she was going to do something about it! She pressed through the crowd, forgetting about what could be said about her. She stretched her physical hand as well as her spiritual hand of faith and she touched Him!

We must realize that many times when we pray, ask and seek; he does not touch us. It could be that He is waiting for us to touch Him and He CAN be touched but only by Faith. Can you SURVIVE THE STRETCHING and receive your miracle? Can you SURVIVE THE STRETCHING and find the cleansing, healing and acceptance that you long for? You sure can! This woman with the issue of blood did. She SURVIVED THE STRETCHING and take notice of what Jesus did for her: *"30 And Jesus, immediately knowing in himself that virtue had gone out of him, turned him about in the press, and said,*

Who touched my clothes? 31 And his disciples said unto him, Thou seest the multitude thronging thee, and sayest thou, Who touched me? 32 And he looked round about to see her that had done this thing. 33 But the woman fearing and trembling, knowing what was done in her, came and fell down before him, and told him all the truth. 34 And he said unto her, Daughter, thy faith hath made thee whole; go in peace, and be whole of thy plague."

This woman was able to go in peace, knowing that her life was changed. Friend, I know that God wants to do the same thing for you. He wants to radically transform life as you know it and make it something beautiful, but you must be willing to touch Him! STRETCH your faith and watch God honor that faith as He did this woman. I believe that you can still hear Him say: *"Thy faith hath made thee whole; go in peace and be whole of thy plague."*

CHAPTER 5
Through the Roof

Have you ever felt like you were about to go "through the roof?" The old saying goes that "when it rains it pours" and if you aren't careful, the troubles of this life will overwhelm you, raise your blood pressure, wreck your nerves and send you "through the roof!" But I have good news for you! You don't have to go "through the roof" in the same way that you used to. You don't have to lose your temper and blow your stack, say or do things that you will regret later. If you can do some stretching, you can go through the roof another way and be glad that you did! If you can SURVIVE THE STRETCHING and you are willing to go "through the roof," I believe that you will find out that God's ways are higher than your ways and that He also has a miracle waiting for you!

The Gospel of Mark affords us an exciting story of a man that had to go "through the roof" to get what he needed from the Lord. The story is recorded in Mark, Chapter 2, beginning at the first verse. Jesus is entering into Capernaum *again*. Notice the word *again*, signifying that Jesus had already been there once before. Before we get too far, I think it would be beneficial to look at what Mark has to say in Chapter 1.

Chapter 1 is action-packed beginning with the ministry of John the Baptist and by verse 14, Jesus is introduced as *"preaching the Gospel of the Kingdom of God."* Mark recounts how Jesus calls Simon and Andrew, followed by James and John (the sons of Zebedee) in verses 16 through 20. At verse 21, Jesus' first trip into Capernaum is recorded as He enters the city, goes immediately to the synagogue and begins to teach. While teaching, a man cries out that is vexed with an unclean spirit (verse 23). Jesus rebukes the unclean spirit and the man is loosed and set free (verses 25 and 26). Later, He heals Simon's mother in law that was bedridden from a fever, although no one told Him that she was sick (verses 29 through 31). People began to marvel over the things that He had done, and the news of this miracle worker spread throughout the village. By evening, a crowd gathered with people bringing to Him those that were sick and those that were possessed by devils. Jesus healed many of their diseases and delivered many from their possessed state (verses 32 through 34).

Jesus left Capernaum as He felt the call to *"go into the next towns..."* and *"preach there also"* (verse 38). He left Capernaum, taught in the neighboring synagogues and performed miraculous feats. His fame grew so much that He had to stay out in the desert and allow the people to come to Him because He could not go openly into the cities (verse 45). Then we arrive back at Chapter 2, verse 1 *"And again he entered into Capernaum after some days."*

After Some Days

We do not know exactly how long Jesus had been gone from Capernaum, but we do know that the people were anxiously awaiting His arrival. Many times, we are just like that. We have seen the miracles and we have heard His words, but He seems so far from us. Faith requires at times that we will not experience miracles. We may not see signs. We will not feel healed or delivered. But are we willing to wait until our time comes for Him to pass our way again?

Suppose the paralyzed man in our story had heard about all the miracles that Jesus had performed while in Capernaum the first time. Perhaps he heard about how Jesus taught with authority and drove out unclean spirits from the people. Surely, he heard about how Jesus healed Simon Peter's Mother-in-law and about the crowds that were brought to the house where He was. The crowds that came to the house sick and left healed. The crowds that came vexed and afflicted of the devil but left whole and relieved of their oppression. Suppose that the paralyzed man *heard* about all of this but could not do anything about it. And then... just like that Jesus had moved on to preach, teach, heal and deliver in another part of the world. He missed Jesus' first trip to Capernaum, but he would not miss the next time.

Many times we get caught up in talking about the good old days and what God used to do. We must realize that God is in the same business today that He has always been in. We lose our zeal. We lose our excitement. We lose our expectation and anticipation that God is going to hear our prayer, minister to our needs or provide in our situation. We lose our will and determination to get to the Master. You must realize that when it seems that God is a million miles away and doing something for everyone around you, that *"after some days"* He is going to come back to where you are! What are you doing to prepare for the time when God will visit your situation again?

I believe the paralyzed man in our story began to make preparation. He knew that when Jesus came back to Capernaum, he would need help to get to where Jesus was. He probably made arrangements for this group of friends to get him to where Jesus was. It is possible that these men were not friends at all. Maybe these four were associates that he had to pay to carry him to see Jesus. Consider this: it has been *"some days"* since you felt the Lord. *"Some days"* since you had the assurance of His Presence. *"Some days"* since you were confident that He heard your prayers. Are your prepared for the next time He passes your way? No matter how long you have waited, once you know that He is in the house, what are you willing to do about it?

It Was Noised

It was noised that Jesus was back in Capernaum and that He was *"in the house,"* (Mark 2:1) more than likely the house of Simon Peter where his mother-in-law had been healed previously. It is about time that we start making some noise again! There is plenty of noise in the world but I'm talking about the kind of noise that glorifies God, lifts up the Name of Jesus and draws the sinner, the backslider, the wanderer, the sick, and the oppressed back to the House of God. Our Churches are not meant to be little secretive, private clubs where the social elite show up on Sundays to hear a pretty little sermon and pray a little patty cake prayer! The Church House is a place where Jesus Christ meets with common man and pours out His love, His power and His grace!

With all the advances in technology, it is time that we started making some noise for the Kingdom of God. We can use Facebook, Twitter and even Instagram to declare the goodness of God. The devil has had these social media platforms for too long! We have allowed it to be used for politics and private agendas, sexual immorality and even an avenue for cyberbullying and unnecessary drama and confusion. Let's take back what we have allowed the devil to use for evil and make some noise for the Kingdom of God!

No Room

All this noise did create a problem, at least for the paralyzed man. Verse 2 says *"And straightway many were gathered together, insomuch that there was no room to receive them, no, not so much as about the door:"* The report that Jesus was back in town created a stirring. People piled into the house where He was. So many people showed up that there was no room even around the door for people to come in. The crowd has always been a problem. As we saw in the last chapter, with the woman with the issue of blood, sometimes we must press through the crowd and as we will see with Zacchaeus, sometimes we have to get ahead of the crowd. As if it isn't enough that this man is crippled by paralysis and has to be carried where he needs to go, they have now run into another problem. Once they get to the house where Jesus is, the crowd is so large, they cannot get the paralyzed man into the house.

Most people would give up and quit because of the crowd. After all, you have heard that "the Church is full of hypocrites" but so is our favorite grocery store. We don't let that keep us from shopping. We've also heard it said that "those people down there are so judgmental" but couldn't we say that same thing about family? But we don't stay home from the family reunions and holiday gatherings. "I just don't fit in at a Church" you might say. The obese man doesn't fit in at the gym, but it might be the best place for him! DO NOT ALLOW PEOPLE TO KEEP YOU FROM JESUS! People will try to crowd you out! They will put their needs, their problems and even their selfish motives ahead of your situation. But again, I say, DO NOT ALLOW PEOPLE TO KEEP YOU FROM JESUS!

This man and his associates did not allow the crowd to keep them from getting what they needed from the Lord… It was time to do something, even something radical to get where they needed to go!

Borne of Four

It is in verse 3 that the paralyzed man enters the scene and Mark notes that he *"was borne of four,"* meaning that he was lifted and carried by four other people. I cannot move past this statement without declaring to you that how far you go with the Lord is many times influenced by the people that you surround yourself with. If you surround yourself with people that could care less about godliness, faith or growing in the Lord, you will not get far. If you surround yourself with those that love the Lord, strive to please Him, believe His word and wait patiently on Him, you will go further than you could have ever imagined. I am thankful for the people that lifted me up and carried me when I was newly converted. I am eternally grateful for the saints that saw me struggle, picked me up and helped me to keep going when I was weak in my faith. Make sure that you know what kind of people you are surrounded by and if they are willing to bear you up and get you closer to the life that you can enjoy only by being in His presence!

There are "Four Friends" that you need if you ever expect to get "through the roof." If you can identify these four qualities in yourself and in the people that you surround yourself with, you will benefit greatly in your endeavors to get to Jesus!

1. Hope

Hope is an essential friend during troubled times. Instead of negativity, doom, gloom, doubt and despair, Hope offers the promise of joy in the morning after a night of tears! (See Psalm 30:5). Hope offers sunshine after the rain. Hope precedes the reception of every good gift from the Father. Without the hope of acceptance and salvation, the sinner man would never turn to God. Without the hope of being healed, the sick man would never seek out the Great Physician. Without the hope of a miracle, would any of us stretch our hand to this Great Miracle Worker? Hope is the joyful expectation of something pleasant or beneficial up ahead.

Job recognized Hope in his pitiful predicament even when he felt there was no hope for him. In Job 14:7, he made the statement *"For there is hope of a tree, if it be cut down, that it will sprout again, and that the tender branch thereof will not cease."* While Job felt that he had been cut down and would never come out of his condition, he knew that God could restore life to even a stump if He chose. If God gives Hope to a stump, imagine the Hope available to His prized creation!

The Psalmist recognized Hope in his hour of depression and desperation. In Psalm 42, his soul was cast down he was facing inner turmoil. He encouraged himself with these words: *"Hope thou in God."* (See Psalm

42:5,11). Everything and everyone else might have left you feeling abandoned and neglected but Hope will point you back to God!

Abraham leaned on this Hope when that is all he had to lean on concerning receiving the promise of God. His body was feeble and his companion was skeptical but he *"against hope believed in hope, that he might become the father of many nations, according to that which was spoken, So shall thy seed be"* (Romans 4:18). The odds were not in Abraham's favor, but he believed in Hope regarding the promise that God had made to him!

This man sick with palsy had at least one friend filled with Hope that things could get better. That friend helped carry the paralyzed man to the One that could perform a miracle! We all need that Friend of Hope and if you cannot find a Friend of Hope, strive to be a man or woman of Hope. Dig into the Word of God and fill your mind and heart with its promises. *"For whatsoever things were written aforetime were written for our learning, that we through patience and comfort of the scriptures might have **Hope**"* (Romans 15:4). The Scriptures are given to us that we might have Hope! Hope is a necessity if you plan to stretch and get to where you need to be. Hope does not work alone. It must be coupled with a Friend called Faith!

2. Faith

You cannot have Faith without Hope because *"faith is the substance of things hoped for, the evidence of things not seen"* (Hebrews 11:1). Faith takes hold of the things that Hope presents to us. Hope makes something a possibility. Faith makes it a reality. Hebrews 11 is filled with men and women that accomplished things in the Lord that could have only been possible through Faith.

Noah had Faith right beside him as he built an ark at God's command. This was a project that did not make sense to humanity at that time for it had never rained, only misted from the ground. Nonetheless, Noah found grace in the eyes of God and received Hope that he and his family would be spared from the coming judgment. He obediently followed God's instruction *"to the saving of his house"* (Hebrews 11:7).

Abraham had Faith when God called him out from his homeland, and he responded with obedience. He and Sara both operated in Faith to bring about the conception of their promised seed from the Lord. (See Hebrews 11:8-12).

Faith was present when Moses' mother put him in a little ark made from bulrushes and placed him down in the river to be discovered by Pharaoh's daughter. But Faith was also present when Moses stepped out of the luxury of Pharaoh's house and identified himself with God's people. This choice ended his comfort and brought about persecution and trouble yet he chose *"rather to suffer affliction with the people of God, than to enjoy the pleasures of sin for a season;"* (Hebrews 11:25).

Without Faith it is impossible to please God and anyone that comes *"to Him must **BELIEVE** (have Faith)* *that He is and that He is a rewarder of them that diligently seek Him!"* (See Hebrews 11:6). Hope reveals the open door of opportunity, but Faith causes us to move toward the door! Surround yourself with people of Faith and make every attempt to build your Faith! How do we do that? *"So then faith cometh by hearing, and hearing by the word of God"* (Romans 10:17). As with Hope, the Word of God produces Faith in the heart of those that hear it and receive it!

3. Prayer

The man with palsy had another friend named Prayer. Hope is the friend that expects something good is up ahead. He sees the open door. Faith believes and produces action. Faith moves toward the open door. But this third friend called Prayer is necessary to receive a miracle. Prayer is ineffective without Faith, but Faith is disorganized and clumsy without Prayer. Prayer seeks guidance and taps into the resources needed to get to that open door.

Prayer was a constant companion in the life of Jesus. It was normal for Jesus to slip away from the crowds to pray, sometimes even spending the entire night in prayer (see Luke 6:12). His prayer life was so remarkable that his disciples would say after hearing Him pray *"Lord teach us to pray"* (Luke 11:1). Prayer was necessary in the life and ministry of Jesus and it must be of the utmost importance in the life of believers today.

This friend named Prayer was with Jeremiah as he was *"shut up in the court of the prison"* (Jeremiah 33:1). While in this despairing predicament, God sends Jeremiah a word! *"Call unto me, and I will answer thee, and shew thee great and mighty things, which thou knowest not"* (Jeremiah 33:3). God was letting Jeremiah know that Prayer was a friend that could be with you in the lowliest of conditions and make available to you things that you could not even imagine!

David was familiar with Prayer as you can see clearly from his writings in the Psalms. In Psalm 18:6, he would write, *"In my distress I called upon the Lord and cried unto my God: he heard my voice out of His temple, and my cry came before Him, even into His ears."* Prayer was with David in his darkest moments. Even from a cave, David would write *"I cried unto the Lord with my voice; with my voice unto the Lord did I make my supplication"* (Psalm 142:1). I believe David would tell us, "No matter what you are going through, take Prayer with you!" Prayer, when coupled with Faith, brings your broken heart, your worries, your anxieties, your confusion directly to the feet of Jesus. And the best part is, that God hears, and He answers!

Hope excitedly anticipates that something good lies ahead. It sees the possibility of an open door. Faith believes and takes action. Faith makes the possibility a reality and makes progress toward the door. But it takes Prayer to connect with God and gain the guidance and the things needed to get to the door. Prayer will tell you which roads to travel, which methods to use. Prayer makes essential resources available such as wisdom, strength and patience. Prayer will also connect you with a friend called Persistence.

4. Persistence

Sometimes Hope, Faith and Prayer are not enough to reach your miracle. There are times that we see the door is open before us through Hope. We believe the door is open for us and we march toward the goal through Faith. The channel of communication with God is clear, petitions have been made and resources have been received through Prayer. Then, as we reach that open door, we discover that some obstacle, some hindrance or some stumbling block now lies in our way. This is where most people give up. This is where the miracle, once like precious fruit hanging on the vine, dries up and dies right in front of us. We hoped, we believed, and we even prayed but we have not persisted! This man, sick of the palsy, borne of four would have died in his condition BUT he had a friend called Persistence!

Persistence was with Blind Bartimaeus as Jesus was leaving out of Jericho. He had heard that Jesus was passing by and *"he began to cry out, and say, Jesus, thou Son of David, have mercy on me."* (See Mark 10:47). This must have upset the religious crowd and the self-seekers that were following Jesus. *"Many charged him that he should hold his peace"* (Mark 10:48). In other words, they tried to shut him up. This is where Persistence steps in! When outside forces, whether they be friends, family, co-workers, church affiliations or satan himself, try to shut us up, we have an important decision to make. Will you give in to popular opinion and the path of least resistance or will you grab Persistence by the hand and pray a little harder? Will you embrace Persistence and allow him to push you to keep stretching, believing, serving and seeking until you receive from God? Blind Bartimaeus followed the urging of Persistence and *"criedthe more a great deal, Thou Son of David, have mercy on me"* (Mark 10:48). Persistence gets the attention of God! *"Jesusstood still and commanded him to be called"* (Mark 10:49). Bartimaeus threw aside his beggarly garments, arose and went to Jesus. Jesus asked and Bartimaeus made his request plain: *"that I might receive my sight"* (Mark 10:51). Jesus granted his request and Bartimaeus left his begging and followed Jesus!

Jesus illustrated how Persistence works with a parable in Luke 18:1-5. He told of a judge that did not fear God and did not regard man. He then told of a widow in the same city that came to the judge with a request: *"Avenge me of mine adversary"* (Luke 18:3). Apparently, she had been wronged in some way and was seeking justice and thus petitioned this judge to avenge her. This judge was a hard man with no consideration for the Righteous Judge above him nor forthe common man he was setover to serve. The differencewith this woman was that she had a friend named Persistence and while most people would have let the matter go, Persistence would not! The judge said *"withinhimself, Though I fear not God, nor regard man, yet because this widow troubleth me, I will avenge her, lest by her continual coming* (Persistence) *she weary me"* (Luke 18:4,5).

The lesson is that Persistence in prayer will take you where prayer alone will not!

Matthew 15 records the story of a Canaanite Woman that had a big problem but no ancestral ties to God's Chosen People, Israel. Although she was entitled to nothing, she had what it took to get through to the Master. She came to Jesus in verse 22 with a request: *"Have mercy on me, O Lord, thou Son of David; my daughter is grievously vexed with a devil."* Strangely, Jesus does not answer her and the disciples wanted to send her away. When Jesus does speak, his response is loaded with rejection: *"I am not sent but unto the lost sheep of the house of Israel"* (Matthew 15:24). Jesus was basically telling her that He had not come to help people of her nationality and background. However, Persistence would not allow the woman to stop there. She worships Him and again entreats Him: *"Lord, help me"* (Matthew 15:25). Again, Jesus answers her with rejection and even a hint of insult: *"It is not meet to take the children's bread, and to cast it to dogs"* (Matthew 15:26). Still, Persistence would not let this heartbroken mother go home with the same issue she came with. She addresses the Lord's rejections by saying *"Truth, Lord: yet the dogs eat of the crumbs which fall from their masters' table"* (Matthew 15:27). Persistence was key in stretching the woman's faith to where she could receive the deliverance that her daughter so desperately needed. Verse 28 says *"Then Jesus answered and said unto her; O woman, great is thy faith: be it unto thee even as thou wilt. And her daughter was made whole from that very hour."*

Hope, Faith and Prayer are all necessary elements in receiving from God but when the door is blocked and there seems to be no way through, Persistence is key! Persistence is what spotted the ladder which lead to the roof. Persistence is what STRETCHED rung after rung of that ladder and hoisted that paralyzed man onto the roof. Persistence is what pulled back the roofing and lowered his friend down to Jesus! Persistence will get you into the building even when the door is blocked!

Uncovering the Roof

These four friends were able to get the paralytic man on top of the roof but what happens next shows us that at times, we all must do things that are uncomfortable or unconventional to get to Jesus. There comes a time when we must decide that we must get into His presence, and we are not going to let anything get in our way. Hope, Faith, Prayer and Persistence got the paralyzed man to the house. They even got him up the ladder. Those four friends got him to the place where only the roof stood between him and Jesus. The natural mind would say it is foolish to tear up a man's roof. The natural mind thinks that it is madness to open the ceiling and let a mandown. The natural mind would think to go home and accept the fact that you are paralyzed. Accept the fact that you will always be like you are. Accept the fact thatyou came close, but you still did not reach the Master. But I am glad that we do not have to settle with the thoughts of our natural mind. We can operate and live in the SUPERnatural realm, where we accept nothing less than God's perfect will!

Beware! Operating in the supernatural will not win you the favor of the world. It comes with consequences. Some will think that you are out of your mind. Others may even be outraged by the things you do. Can you imagine the owner of the home where Jesus was? As he saw the fragments falling and the straw and clay tile being broken up and pulled away? He more than likely was not a happy camper with what he saw! Are you willing to be despised? Are you willing to be ridiculed? Laughed at? Talked about? You must certainly prepare yourself *"because the carnal mind is enmity against God: for it is not subject to the law of God, neither indeed can be"* (Romans 8:7). As you draw closer to the Lord and become more spiritually minded, those that are fleshly minded will not comprehend and will surely attack that which they do not understand.

Regardless of the attack; regardless of the ridicule; regardless of the misconceptions, the roof MUST come off if you are going to get to Jesus. I am not suggesting that we have to go around being destructive or tearing down peoples' personal property. The roof is merely symbolic of the barrier between where we are and the Presence of the Lord. Many things hold us back from deeper depths in the Spirit. Pride is a problem for so many people but *"God resisteth the proud"* and He *"giveth grace to the humble"* (James 4:6, 1 Peter 5:5). Pride may be the "roof" that God is waiting on you to break up and get out of the way. Sin is another possibility. Isaiah declared in Chapter 59, verses 1 and 2: *"Behold, the LORD'S hand is not shortened, that it cannot save; neither His ear heavy, that it cannot hear: 2 But your iniquities have separated between you and your God, and your sins have hid His face from you, that He will not hear."* Sin could very well be the roof that is separating you from His Presence! Unforgiveness is a hidden obstacle, sometimes lying dormant in the heart of a man for decades. Life is full of hurt, pain, betrayal and abuse but as Believers, we are compelled to forgive our offender no matter how terrible the offense is. Forgiveness clears the soul and releases unnecessary baggage from the heart. It always removes the "roof" of unforgiveness that keeps us from reaching Jesus. Remember what Jesus said in Matthew 6:14, 15 *"For if ye forgive men their trespasses, your heavenly Father will also forgive you: 15 But if ye forgive not men their trespasses, neither will your Father forgive your trespasses."*

The question is: Are you willing to tear the roof off to get to Jesus???

Thy Sins Be Forgiven Thee

After uncovering a part of the roof, the paralytic man is lowered down into the Presence of the Lord. Those friends STRETCH out ropes or some type of material and create a holstering system and attached it to the man's bed. They stretch until they get the man down to where Jesus is. Verse 5 says that *"Jesus saw their faith."* Faith will always be evidenced by something that we can see. *"Even so faith, if it hath not works, is dead, being alone. 18 Yea, a man may say, Thou hast faith, and I have works: shew me thy faith without thy works, and I will shew thee my faith by my works"* James 2:17, 18. Faith and works go hand in hand and if we genuinely have faith, it can be seen, just as Jesus saw the faith of this man and his friends. However, when He sees their faith, He does not address the obvious problem of paralysis. Jesus overlooks the mat that he was lowered down on. He ignores the crippled legs and he looks deeper into the soul of this man. He says to the man *"Son, thy sins be forgiven thee."* Again, the natural mind would say "I did not come here for this. I came here for healing. I came here because I am paralyzed." Jesus, the same today as He was in Mark, Chapter 2, is not concerned primarily with the physical. He is concerned about the soul.

The work of salvation is an inside job. The work of healing is an inside job. The work of the miraculous is an inside job. When God begins a good work in a man, He starts on the inside. He focuses on that which is most important, the soul of man. At this point, if the paralytic man had left the house, he would have everything he ever needed: salvation from sin and peace with God! What is it that you need from God? Is it provision? Is it physical healing? Is there some force oppressing you, keeping you from walking and going forward in life? Maybe your issue is deeper than the surface manifestations. This is the area that Jesus deals with first. *"Son, thy sins be forgiven thee"* cured the man's most detrimental disease: sin and separation from God. In just a few words, Jesus had spoken peace to a sin-tossed soul and gave the man a cure that could not have been provided by any doctor.

Whatever it is that you are dealing with during the stretching process, be mindful that God wants to first deal with the inner issues. Are you born again? Do you have peace with God? Is your heart, soul and mind resting in His care and trusting in His word? Until these questions have been answered, any other work is a temporary fix.

The Son of Man Hath Power

Of course, Jesus' authority to forgive sins created a stir among the religious people. Verses 6 and 7 state that *"there were certain of the scribes sitting there, and reasoning in their hearts, 7 Why doth this man thus speak blasphemies? who can forgive sins but God only?"* Things are not much different today. The religious may not question his ability to forgive sins, but they are quick to decide who should be forgiven and who should not. They do not hesitate to judge which sins and which sinners are redeemable and worthy to be forgiven. The truth is, Christ and Christ alone has authority among men to forgive sins. Jesus knew the hearts of the scribes that were there and He goes on to say *"Why reason ye these things in your hearts? 9 Whether is it easier to say to the sick of the palsy, Thy sins be forgiven thee; or to say, Arise, and take up thy bed, and walk? 10 But that ye may know that the Son of man hath power on earth to forgive sins"* (Mark 2:8-10). Jesus took this situation as an opportunity to display His authority, not just over demonic forces and physical sicknesses, but also over sin. To us, there may seem to be a significant difference between sickness and sin but to Jesus, it is just as easy to tell the sinner they are forgiven as it is for Him to tell the paralyzed man to get up and walk. Thank God that Jesus Christ has power on earth! Not just to heal the sick. Not just to speak peace to the storm. Not just to drive out unclean spirits. He also has power on earth to forgive sins! What a blessed assurance!

Arise

Jesus does not forget about the paralytic man and his crippled condition. Jesus turns back to him and says in verse 11: *"I say unto thee, Arise, and take up thy bed, and go thy way into thine house."* Once the inner issues are dealt with, sins are forgiven, and our soul has been reconciled we can expect Jesus to perform the miraculous. The very things that we NEED are His good pleasure to give to us. He expounded on this thought in His teaching in Luke 12. Here is a portion of that passage that expresses His great love to meet our needs: *"And seek not ye what ye shall eat, or what ye shall drink, neither be ye of doubtful mind. 30 For all these things do the nations of the world seek after: and your Father knoweth that ye have need of these things. 31 But rather seek ye the kingdom of God; and all these things shall be added unto you. 32 Fear not, little flock; for it is your Father's good pleasure to give you the kingdom"* (Luke 12:29-32). Just as boldly as Jesus had forgiven the man's sins, He would now meet the man's physical need and heal his body!

In His instruction to get up and walk, Jesus also tells the man to take up his bed (the mat that he had been lying on) and go home. This mat represented a lot of pain and heartache. It symbolized his years of paralysis. It was a reminder of his inability to work, play and join in on festivities and celebrations. Jesus tells him to take the very thing that most of us would want to leave behind. This would be a great testimony to all that saw him carried one way and now walking on his way back home. *"And immediately he arose, took up the bed, and went forth before them all; insomuch that they were all amazed, and glorified God, saying, We never saw it on this fashion"* (Mark 2:12). What a testimony you will be for the world to see if you can SURVIVE THE STRETCHING! You can be a testimony of His Grace as He forgives your sins and a testimony of His love and power as He restores the crippled, paralyzed places of your life!

CHAPTER 6
Seeking from the Sycamore Tree

What would you do to experience the Lord? How far would you be willing to go to have an encounter with Jesus? Would you be willing to leave your comfort zone and do something out of the ordinary to receive a visitation with God? Unfortunately, so many people feel like God would never ask them to do something uncomfortable. Even many Christians feel like their walk with the Lord should be a comfortable stroll with no bumps, bends or burdens. However, the Word of God is filled with Men and Women who encountered God, experienced great victories and received extraordinary blessings, but it often costed them. Some had to give up luxuries and comfort, like Moses did. Some had to stand toe to toe with giants, as David did. Some had to step out of the boat and do the impossible, like Peter did. And some had to stretch their legs and climb a tree... like Zacchaeus did. It may seem unnatural. It may seem uncomfortable. It may even seem unreasonable, but as we read the story of Zacchaeus, we will find it is always worthwhile to seek the Lord even if we must stretch ourselves to seek Him from a sycamore tree! There is no telling what may happen if you SURVIVE THE STRETCHING!

A Picture of Zacchaeus

We find the story of Zacchaeus recorded in Luke, Chapter 19. The Bible tells us that Jesus had *"entered and passed through Jericho"* (Luke 19:1) and His arrival caught the attention of a man by the name of Zacchaeus, *"which was the chief among the publicans, and he was rich"* (Luke 19:2). This description is not becoming at all. It essentially reveals two strikes against Zacchaeus. The first is this: He was chief among the publicans. Simply put, he was a tax collector and no one is particularly fond of tax collectors. The second strike against Zacchaeus was that he was rich. It wasn't just the fact that he was wealthy but that his wealth was connected to his occupation. He had accumulated his wealth from collecting taxes and possibly doing it at a rate that abused the people for his personal benefit. The third strike against poor Zacchaeus is revealed to us in verse 3: *"he was little of stature."*

It has been presumed and often preached that Zacchaeus was a short man. This is possible but not certain. The fact that *"he was little of stature"* could of course mean that he was of little height. Another possibility could be his age. It could be that Zacchaeus was a young man, little in terms of age and maturity. The third possibility is that this could be a reference to his reputation or his standing in the community. It could be that he was of lowly reputation because of his occupation. No matter which possibility is correct, the fact is, Zacchaeus had three strikes against him. He was a rich man with a lucrative position, but he was still lacking something. That void drove him as *"he sought to see Jesus who he was"* (Luke 19:3).

The Press

Zacchaeus already has these three strikes against him but now he is presented with a problem as he strives to see Jesus. He *"could not for the press"* (Luke 19:3). We have already seen how "the press" made it difficult for the woman with the issue of blood to reach Jesus in Mark, Chapter 5. We read how the crowd made it impossible for the paralytic man to get in the house with Jesus in Mark, Chapter 2. "The press" here again creates an issue as Zacchaeus makes an effort to see Jesus. "The press" will always be an issue when seeking the Lord. Hypocrites will always be present in the Church. Critics, mockers and scoffers will always be connected to us in some way. Negative voices are always going to speak out from the multitudes around us. All of this is true. It has always been true, and it will always be true as long as we are among the living. But we do not have to let this issue keep us from seeing Jesus. "The press" may be a stumbling block but it does not have to be a brick wall. You can always do like Zacchaeus did! Verse 4 tells us that *"he ran before."* Zacchaeus made up his mind that the crowd may squeeze him out from getting on the front line, but they were not going to keep him from seeing the Lord. He took off running! Are you willing to run and get ahead of your problems? When the devil tries to block your view and people get in your way, will you sit there and sulk or get up and run ahead? Zacchaeus decided to run!

The Sycamore Tree

Not only did Zacchaeus run ahead of the crowd but he *"climbed up into a sycamore tree"* because he knew that Jesus *"was to pass that way"* (Luke 19:4). As Christians, we often talk about how we want to be closer with the Lord. We talk about how we want to pray more. We talk about how we want to study more. We talk about how we want to do more in our communities to be a light for Jesus. The sad thing is that many of our well-intentioned plans die right there, while we are talking about it. Zacchaeus had heard about Jesus, purposed in his heart that he would go out and see Him as he passed by but ran into the problem with the crowd surrounding Jesus. He very well could have gone home and talked about how he longed to see Jesus but it didn't happen. He could have stayed on the outskirts of the crowd, talking about how he would love to get closer. But we do not see him saying anything here. He has a sincere desire to see Jesus and does something about it. He calculates the route that Jesus would surely take, runs ahead and finds a sycamore tree to climb up in so that he can simply see

Jesus as he passes by. Are we that devoted to stretch our faith and stretch our legs to run and then... climb???

Unfortunately, a form of Christianity is on the rise today that we will refer to as Casual Christianity. This Casual Christianity does not require that you do anything more than find a good Church and attend when it is convenient. Casual Christianity puts no stress or discomfort on its followers. To join a Church, maybe give a little, or volunteer a little, is the pinnacle of the Casual Christian experience. No manifestations of His Glory. No intimate experiences through times of tarrying in prayer. No hearing or discerning of the Lord's voice and direction for their personal life. Simply attending, giving and volunteering when or if it is convenient. But there is so much more in the Christian experience! There is a personal, intimate relationship with our Risen Savior! There is joy unspeakable and power inconceivable in His presence! There is healing and soothing for the body and spirit as we walk with Him and talk with Him, not only on Sundays or special occasions but every day if we are willing!

But we must be willing! Willing to stretch and climb the sycamore tree. Isaiah said that if we were willing and obedient, we could enjoy the privilege of eating the good of the land (Isaiah 1:19)! Now, can you imagine Zacchaeus, especially if he was truly a man of little height, stretching his legs, one limb at a time? One tug at a time, pulling himself up high enough to see Jesus? He was willing and he was hungry just to SEE Jesus; but he received so much more than that.

The Place

Verse 5 says *"And when Jesus came to the place..."* What place? He came to the place where Zacchaeus was. He knew exactly where Zacchaeus was. Zacchaeus had climbed that tree to see Jesus, but he did not expect that Jesus was also looking forward to seeing him. The amazing thing about Jesus is that He never meets a man that He does not already know the state of that man. You may be saying, "I cannot come to Jesus because I have done too much wrong." Or "Jesus would never accept me where I am right now." Many people feel like they must reform who they are before coming to Jesus. They erroneously feel like they must quit smoking, drinking, using foul language and end immoral relationships. They also look to break habits, quit going to certain places and THEN come to Jesus. Brother, Sister, this could not be further from the truth! If you were able to do all these things, you would not need Jesus or His transforming grace. Come to Jesus just as you are and He will take the cigarettes, the drugs, the alcohol, the profanity, the sexual immorality. He will break the habits and heal the broken places. He will take away your bitterness, your unforgiveness, your prejudice and your anger. He will change the course of your day, the people you hang out with and the places that you go. Jesus knows where you are. He knows what you have done. And He comes to the place... He comes to the place where you are!

Jesus *"looked up and saw him, and said unto him, Zacchaeus..."* (Luke 19:5) Jesus called Zacchaeus BY

NAME. He needed no formal introduction. He did not have to whisper to His disciples to investigate who this man was up in the sycamore tree. Jesus knows ALL about you. Not only what you have done and where you are, but He knows you better than YOU know YOU. He knows WHO you are, and He calls you out by name. He knows your identity, no matter how well you may hide it from the world around you. God told Jeremiah *"Before I formed thee in the belly I knew thee;"* (Jeremiah 1:5). God knew Jeremiah and called him before he was ever conceived. And in the same way, God knew Zacchaeus. How amazing that before that sycamore tree ever sprouted from a seed, God knew Zacchaeus! Before Zacchaeus was ever thought of, God knew Zacchaeus. And in the same way, God knows you! He knew that you would come to the place where you are, and He comes to you in that place and He calls you by name because He knows you. And even though He knows you, He loves you. He knows about your bad attitude. He knows about your ungodly desires and greed. He knows about your moments of selfishness and shameful weakness. HE KNOWS YOU! Yet, in the way that only He can, He loves you unconditionally. And He loves you too much to leave you the way you are. Now, if you will heed His calling and follow His instructions, He will change you in the way that only He can.

Salvation and the Effects

From this point, forward, we see a domino effect in Zacchaeus' behavior. As you will see, salvation is a process that begins as we respond to the call of Jesus. It is a process. It is not merely an emotional response that we have after hearing a sermon or a song that moves us from our seat. Too often, sinners respond to the Gospel and we consider them "saved" but never challenge them to continue. Salvation will NEVER leave you where God found you. Salvation is the lamb being brought back into the fold by a loving Shepherd. Salvation is the house being swept and cleaned and a lost coin that is restored to its rightful place. Salvation is a prodigal son that squandered everything coming to his senses and returning home, having a ring placed on his finger, new shoes on his feet and a clean robe to cover him. Salvation is manifested in a man named Zacchaeus, coming down from the sycamore tree and welcoming Jesus not only into his home but into his personal life and being transformed. Jesus Himself would go on to say, *"This day is salvation come to this house"* (Luke 19:9).

Before we close this chapter, let us look at Zacchaeus and how his salvation began to immediately transform him. We see four things in the life of Zacchaeus that we should see clearly in our own experience of salvation and how the grace and love of God compel us to be different!

1. Obedience

Upon looking up and seeing Zacchaeus in the tree, Jesus gives him a simple instruction: *"Zacchaeus, make haste, and come down; for to day I must abide at thy house"* (Luke19:5). Many complain that His instructions are too hard and too difficult to carry out but I must agree with what Solomon said in Proverbs 13:15 "... *the way of transgressors is hard*" and with what Jesus said in Matthew 11:30 "*For my yoke is easy, and my burden is light.*" Sin is hard. It has pleasure for a season, but it is a hard life! Jesus, on the other hand, gives simple instructions for living and in comparison to the hard lifeof the sinner, His yoke is easy!

Then, there are others, even among Christians that feel like there is no need for instruction or discipline in the Christian life. But Jesus said this: "*If ye love me, keep my commandments*" (John 14:15). True Repentance (turning away from sin, ungodliness and fleshliness andturning to God) leads to Salvation (deliverance from those very things that we are turning away from). Salvation leads us into deeper and deeper depths of loveand adoration for the Savior. There are many things in the Word of God that naturally, we would not want to do. However, once we are saved or born again, our desires begin to change. We begin to WANT to do the very things that we once hated and likewise we begin tohate the things that we once wanted to do.

The first product of Salvation is Obedience. Because we love Him, our desire to please Him and serve Him continues to increase. His first instruction to Zacchaeus was to "*make haste, and come down*" in verse 5. His obedience to that command is recorded in verse 6 "*And he made haste, and came down.*" He did exactly what Jesus said and did it exactly how Jesus said to do it. To the lost person and even some professing Christians, the Bible looks like a book full of stringent rules and regulations that they want no part of. To the Born-Again Believer, we see the Word of God as a book full of instruction and directions on how to live a good life in this world and one that will please our Savior. And as a Believer, we now strive to be as obedient as we can to the things recorded in this blessed book!

2. Joy

Verse 6 goes on to say that Zacchaeus not only *"made haste and came down"* but also that *"he received Him joyfully."* One of the marks of a man that has come to know the Lord is joy! After conversion, a man still has and will have much improving to do until the day that he goes home to meet the Lord. We will never be perfect until we get to that heavenly shore. But a change does occur at Salvation. Salvation changes our nature. If you were a sad person before conversion, you now have a reason to smile. If you were an angry person before conversion, you now have a reason to lay down that hurt and anger and bitterness. If you were a happy person before conversion, you now know the fullness of joy through Jesus Christ! In Acts 8, we see Philip going down to the city of Samaria and preaching to them the Good News of Christ. As a result, the demon-possessed were set free and the sick were healed. Verse 8 says *"And there was great joy in that city."* A sure-fire way to tell that Christ has been accepted is that there will be *"great joy in that city."*

The second product of Salvation is Joy! Through the blood of Jesus Christ and His redeeming work at Calvary, you have been granted access to His most Holy Presence! Hebrews 10:19-20 says that we have *"boldness to enter into the holiest by the blood of Jesus, 20 by a new and living way, which He hath consecrated for us, through the veil, that is to say, his flesh."* This boldness that we have is a confidence that we can come into His Presence and is only made available through the shed blood of Jesus and His broken flesh. His Presence, so often taken for granted, is the source of healing, peace, security, and yes, JOY! (See Psalm 16:11). A man cannot enter the Presence of God and leave the same as he entered. Circumstances and situations in life can and will cause all sorts of strains, discomforts and even discontent, but our Salvation produces something that the world cannot take away: Joy! For whatever ails you, accept His love, dwell in His Presence, receive His joy! Jesus said "These things have I spoken unto you, that my joy might remain in you, and that your joy might be full" John 15:11. He has left us His Word, His instructions and promises that HIS joy could remain in us and that OUR joy could be full!

3. Good Works/Charity

Jesus went home with Zacchaeus, being criticized by the religious crowd for being the *"guest with a man that is a sinner"* (Luke 19:7). Thankfully, Jesus still comes to sinners and receives us as we are or none of us would stand a chance. In verse 8 *"Zacchaeus stood, and said unto the Lord; Behold, Lord, the half of my goods I give to the poor."* The third thing that Zacchaeus did upon his encounter with Jesus was to pledge an effort to reach out to those less fortunate than himself. A heart that truly receives the Lord will lean toward good works and blessing those around them.

There are many misconceptions about good works and salvation. Many people feel like they must do good works to be saved. We must be clear on the fact that there will NEVER be enough that you can do to save yourself or to earn your salvation. You could live a life filled with charity and good works, giving to the poor, feeding the hungry, clothing the naked, and even carry out religious practices such as singing, preaching or teaching and still not make it to heaven! Jesus warned in Matthew 7:21-23 *"Not every one that saith unto me, Lord, Lord, shall enter into the kingdom of heaven; but he that doeth the will of my Father which is in heaven. 22 Many will say to me in that day, Lord, Lord, have we not prophesied in thy name? and in thy name have cast out devils? and in thy name done many wonderful works? 23 And then will I profess unto them, I never knew you: depart from me, ye that work iniquity."* Never forget that we are saved by grace, through faith... ***"NOT OF WORKS,*** *lest any man should boast"* (Ephesians 2:8, 9). There is only one way to Heaven and His name is Jesus: *"Jesus saith unto him,* ***I AM THE WAY,*** *the truth, and the life:* ***NO MAN*** *cometh unto the Father,* ***BUT BY ME"*** (John 14:6). Your good works, charitable donations, good looks, great personality, etc. all fall short of what it takes to save you!

There is another school of thought that says that since we are saved by grace and through faith and not by works, that those good works are not needed. This is also a misconception. While we are not saved BY our good works, we are saved TO DO good works. The same passage that teaches us that we are not saved by good works also teaches us that *"we are His workmanship, created in Christ Jesus **unto good works**, which God hath before ordained that we should walk in them"* (Ephesians 2:10). God created you with a specific purpose in mind and being born again, we are transformed in Christ Jesus to be able to carry out those good works that we were ordained to walk in. Paul also wrote to Titus and encouraged him to *"affirm constantly, that they which have believed in God might be careful to maintain good works. These things are good and profitable unto men"* (Titus 3:8). James would write concerning faith and good works that *"faith, if it hath not works, is dead, being alone"* (James 2:17) and he would go on to pose the challenge *"shew me thy faith without thy works, and I will shew thee my faith by my works"* (James 2:18). Consider the instruction that Jesus gave in Matthew 5:16 *"Let your light so shine before men, that they may see your good works, and glorify your Father which is in heaven."*

4. Restitution

Zacchaeus did not stop with good works and charity for the poor. He went on to say *"If I have taken any thing from any man by false accusation, I restore him fourfold"* (Luke 19:8). This salvation experience with Jesus awoke something within Zacchaeus that made him want to go back and make right the things that he had done wrong. For believers, this is not always possible. Sometimes, the person or people that we have wronged have passed on or we have lost touch with them. But wherever and whenever possible, we should do what we can to make restitution for the wrongs that we have committed. Of course, the man that has made a career out of being a petty thief will never be able to retrace and return all the items that were stolen. The habitual liar will never be able to recall all his or her lies much less the people that were victimized by those lies. The abusive spouse or parent can never take back the damage that they have inflicted on those they were supposed to love. The addict can never make up for the lost sleep and lost peace that they caused their friends and family to endure. However, we can begin with a sincere apology and changed behavior that makes that apology credible.

Restitution is key in living *"peaceably with all men."* Paul said, *"If it be possible, as much as lieth in you, live peaceably with all men"* (Romans 12:18). Many times, the only way we can restore peace in a relationship is by making restitution. We must take ownership of the wrong that we have committed and do so without making excuses. Without dishing blame on anyone else and without justifying ourselves. We must acknowledge that our actions have caused pain or heartache for someone else. And the good news is, Salvation creates this desire within us. The humility and joy of being born again causes it to be no heavy burden to give back what we have taken or to soothe the wounds that we have created. And no sin is too great. No trespass is too terrible. Where sin abounds, God's grace flourishes at an even greater measure (see Romans 5:20)!

Throughout our journey of faith, there will be offenses. Jesus said, *"It is impossible but that offences will come: but woe unto him, through whom they come!"* (See Luke 17:1). How true that verse is, it is impossible to live without offenses but when we are the source of an offense, what woe it causes us, especially as Children of God! The key to limiting offenses is to live according to the rule that Jesus gave us in Matthew 7: 12 *"Therefore all things whatsoever ye would that men should do to you, do ye even so to them: for this is the law and the prophets."* Simply put, live in such a way that you treat others the way that you would like to be treated and by doing this, keeping the law and the instructions of the prophets would be a whole lot easier! And when offenses do come (and they will), make restitution quickly. Resolve those issues before they fester and cause unnecessary grudges or walls that keep us from being effective in our ministry of being a witness for Christ!

This Day Is Salvation Come to This House

Too many times, we have missed what God had prepared for us because we refused to stretch. Zacchaeus started his day as a lowly (wealthy, but lowly) tax collector. He ended his day, having shared his home and a meal with Jesus. Jesus declared that Salvation had come to the house of this man that the rest of the world viewed as "little of stature." Jesus then refers to Zacchaeus as a "son of Abraham" (Luke 19:9), referring to him being a descendant of Abraham, the great man of faith. Up until this point, Zacchaeus' life had been a poor reflection of his connection to the great man of faith, Abraham. This meeting had changed all of that. Zacchaeus' yesterdays were gone, his wrongs were made right and the stain of his sin was washed away. He had been restored to his full potential as a "Son of Abraham." Jesus specializes in those kinds of miracles. That is why He came, "to seek and to save that which was lost" (Luke 19:10). He has done it for millions of souls, and He wants to do it for you and me. Are you willing to SURVIVE THE STRETCHING? Do the uncomfortable? Climb the sycamore tree? If you can SURVIVE THE STRETCHING, you can experience Christ today, just as Zacchaeus did way back then!

CHAPTER 7
Stretch Forth Thine Hand

Every one of us has a withered hand. We have an area (or areas) of weakness in our life. There are two types of people when it comes to the withered hand. Some people flaunt it. They like the attention they get from showing their weakness. These are the type of people that glory in the fact that they can "cuss like a sailor" or "smoke like a chimney." Instead of dealing with their areas of weakness, they make a show out of it, boasting of how many people that have been "involved" with, how many fights they have won, or how drunk they got. Then there is the other group. This group hides that withered hand. They make sure their hair is combed, their shoes are polished, their clothing is tidy and neat, but that withered hand is stuffed into their pocket so that no one can see it. They go to Church; they attend Sunday School. They go to all of the community functions, perform well on their jobs and even volunteer in their spare time. However, they would never want anyone to know, that somewhere hidden from view is a withered hand. But rest assured, whether it is flaunted or hidden, every one of us has a withered hand. It does not matter which category you fall into; Jesus can perform a miracle for you just like He did for the man in Mark, Chapter 3 if you can SURVIVE THE STRETCHING!!!

The Man With the Withered Hand

In Mark, Chapter 3 we find that Jesus *"entered again into the synagogue"* (verse 1) and Luke adds that *"he entered into the synagogue and taught"* (Luke 6:6). On this occasion, there is a man present that has a *"withered hand,"* and again Luke would add more detail by letting us know that *"his right hand was withered"* (Luke 6:6). We can all identify with this man. As it has already been stated, every one of us has a withered hand of some sort. One man may have a short temper. One dear saint may have a gossiping tongue. Another may have a lustful eye. Someone else may battle an addiction. We must learn not to look down our nose at someone else's withered hand just because ours is manifested in another way. We all have these areas of weakness because of our great, great, great, great grandfather Adam. Romans 5:19 says *"For by one man's disobedience, many were made sinners, so by the obedience of One shall many be made righteous."* We all know that Jesus was the ONE that came and was obedient unto the death of the cross so that we could be made righteous. But we cannot forget that when Adam fell in disobedience, he dropped all of mankind. Many were made sinners. Because of that great fall from perfection, Adam and every individual that has sprung from his family tree has some type of shortcoming in their flesh. We call it the Adamic nature, that predisposition to sin. David identified this inbred problem this way: *"Behold, I was shapen in iniquity; and in sin did my mother conceive me"* (Psalm 51:5).

For many of us, in this man, we see a picture of ourselves. We are in the synagogue. We are trying to do right. We go to the right places, try to hang around the right people. But every time we take the time to examine ourselves, we find to our disappointment, that our hand is still withered. We still have that shortcoming, we still have that weakness, we still struggle in some area that makes us feel less than adequate to be the person that God has called us to be. Do not be discouraged, this man's story begins with a withered hand, but it does not end with a withered hand. And if we follow this man's example, our story does not have to end with a withered hand either! We can experience restoration and wholeness if we are willing to stretch our faith and be obedient.

The Man Was There

We take for granted how important it is to be THERE. We do not realize the importance of gathering together with other believers. The letter to the Hebrews included a command that the modern Church needs to be reminded of: *"Not forsaking the assembling of ourselves together, as the manner of some is; but exhorting one another: and so much the more, as ye see the day approaching"* (Hebrews 10:25). In simple terms: DO NOT QUIT ASSEMBLING TOGETHER! It may be culturally acceptable to stay home and watch your favorite preacher or Church by way of TV or the internet but that is no substitute for being THERE!

The man with the withered hand was THERE. That first verse of Chapter 3 says that when Jesus entered the synagogue, *"there was a man THERE which had a withered hand."* He was present in the synagogue at the same time that Jesus was. How many miracles have been missed? How many healings have not been issued? How many deliverances have not been experienced? All because we were not THERE. We did not show up. We did not go to the prayer meeting. We did not go to worship. We did not go to the Bible Study. When God was prepared to do something special, we dropped the ball because we were not THERE! The first key to experiencing anything from God is being THERE and being excited about having the opportunity to be there. David said, *"I was glad when they said unto me, Let us go into the house of the Lord"* (Psalm 122:1).

What a privilege to join with other believers whether it be for worship, prayer, Bible study, or for simple fellowship. Anytime that we gather together in His Name, He has made us a promise: *"For where two or three are gathered together in my name, there am I in the midst of them"* (Matthew 18:20). Never forget that promise! Whether the service was dry and lifeless, or it was full of life and excitement, He is THERE! If you will show up, He is saying to us that He will show up. The withered man was on his way to his miracle simply by being

THERE, being present where the Lord was. That's the first key to whatever you need! BE PRESENT!

They Watched Him

This is just a quick side note to mention that in verse 2, Mark records that *"they watched Him, whether He would heal him on the Sabbath day; and that they might accuse Him."* It is has been noted a few times already that people have always tried to hinder the work of God. It is recorded repeatedly in scripture, whether referred to as "the press" or "the crowd" or here just referred to as "they." "They" refers to the religious leaders; those that were intimidated by Jesus' ministry. "They" had no desire to be healed. "They" had no desire to learn. "They" had no desire to learn of this new way that Jesus was ushering in. "They" simply wanted to watch so that they could find fault and have a reason to accuse Him. Do not be deceived. Times have not changed much. The faces may be different, and the names may be changed but "they" are still among us. "They" are all over the Church world and we cannot allow their spectating, speculating, criticisms to hinder us! Nor can we allow their refusal to receive and respond to keep us from receiving what we need from the Lord!

He Saith To the Man

Being present is one thing but being attentive is another. How many times have we been guilty of being THERE physically but not being there mentally? We showed up for Sunday School, but we could not repeat the memory verse if our life depended on it. We were present at Church, but we could not tell you the songs that were sung or the sermon that was preached. Most people are guilty of being present but not being attentive. If you could read the minds of those that were present at a normal gathering you may find a wide variety of things. Some people are thinking about the ham they left baking back at home. Some people are thinking about where they are going to get lunch after they leave the service. Some people are thinking about a conflict they had with their spouse on the way to Church. Some people are thinking about the way someone else in the Church treated them that morning. Some people are still singing a song they heard on the way to Church. Being present is important but we must go a step further and be attentive.

Verse three says that Jesus spoke to the man. *"And he saith unto the man..."* Jesus is still speaking today. He still gives us nudges and impressions through the Holy Ghost and His Word is just as valid today as it was when He was walking on earth. The problem is that we are not being attentive. Jesus had a few things to say about hearing His voice and recognizing when He speaks to us. Speaking of the relationship between sheep and the shepherd, Jesus said *"4 And when he putteth forth his own sheep, he goeth before them, and the sheep follow him: for they know his voice.5 And a stranger will they not follow, but will flee from him: for they know not the voice of strangers."* (See John 10:4,5). Sheep recognize the voice of their shepherd

108

and we likewise should be able to discern the voice of our Shepherd. Jesus had such confidence in this that He went on to say *"My sheep hear my voice, and I know them, and they follow me:"* (John 10:27). If you have never felt God speaking to you or have never discerned His voice and direction in your life, it is not that God has quit speaking. It is that we have failed to be attentive. Sometimes, we allow the noise of the world to overwhelm us. Too much politics, too many negative news stories, too many gossiping phone calls or too many criticizing skeptics. Many times, we need to mute the noises from around the world so that we may hear the voice of God clearly. You find this even in the life of Jesus. At times, he would get in a boat and launch out from land or steal away early in the morning to pray. He did this so that the distractions and interferences of the world would be limited as He communed with His Father and received direction from Him. This is why Jesus could say in John 5:30 *"I can of mine own self do nothing: as I hear, I judge: and my judgment is just; because I seek not mine own will, but the will of the Father which hath sent me."* Jesus lived a life of holiness, supernatural strength and extraordinary miracles because He carried out that which He received from The Father! How much more could we accomplish and how much more could we experience if we were attentive to the voice of our Shepherd?

Stand Forth

Jesus speaks to the man and this is the instruction that He gives the man with the withered hand: "*Stand forth*" (Mark 3:3). The man is present. The man is attentive. He is in the synagogue at the right time and he is attentive when Jesus speaks to him. But here is the beginning of the true test. Is the man willing to "stand forth"? It was possible that Jesus was not just asking him to stand up, though that would be awkward enough. Another way to translate this term "stand forth" could be to "stand out in the midst" or "stand out in the middle." Jesus was asking this man to stand out, amid the other congregants, in such a way that attention was drawn to this man. Are you willing to stand out? Many times, the plan of God will take you into areas that you are not comfortable. God's plan took Daniel to the lion's den. It took Shadrach, Meshach and Abednego to the fiery furnace. It took Paul and Silas to the prison. It caused many of the disciples to be jailed, beaten, mocked and some even murdered. Jesus spoke to the man to "stand forth" or in other words, step out amid the crowd. Be different. Be separate. Be distinguished from the attenders and the pretenders. If you are going to make any difference in this world for God and if you are going to see the goodness of God in this world, you cannot just float downstream like a dead fish. You must be willing to Stand Up, Stand Forth and Stand Out for Jesus!

Stretch Forth Thine Hand

After dealing with the religious crowd that had shown up just to watch and find fault, Jesus turns back to the man in verse 5 and says, *"Stretch forth thine hand."* So far, the man with the withered hand has laid out for us an excellent pattern for receiving a miracle or experiencing that restorative touch that can only come from the Lord. He was present. He was attentive. He was willing to stand up and stand out according to Jesus' direction. But will he be willing to expose that area of weakness? Jesus was not just asking him to stand out from the crowd anymore. He was asking the man to be transparent; to reveal the very thing that made him a handicap. To expose the area that made him inferior to the rest of the crowd. Is the man willing to be obedient to this degree?

Obedience is better than sacrifice (See 1 Samuel 15:22) and Jesus said *"If ye love me, keep my commandments"* (John 14:15). Our obedience says more about us than our attendance to Church and our financial giving statement! However, obedience is not always easy. Just ask Jonah. He did not want to go to those rebellious people of Nineveh. Obedience looked like a hard road to take but Jonah also found out that disobedience is an even harder road with severe consequences. Are you willing to be obedient to this degree?

The man with the withered hand quickly obeyed what Jesus told him to do. Verse 5 also records his response: *"And he stretched it out."* (Mark 3:5). No matter how humiliating it seemed. No matter how awkward it appeared to be. No matter how many people were watching or if anyone was scoffing or making fun, the man obeyed God! This combined with the other keys laid out by this man's experience lead to a miraculous happening that day! He was present! He was attentive! He was willing to stand out! And when it came time, he was obedient!

His Hand Was Restored

This man stretched out his hand just as he was instructed and as he did, something amazing began to take place. For whatever reason, this man's hand had become withered, shriveled or dried up. He may have been born this way, with a hand that he was never able to use. Perhaps there was some sort of accident that caused his hand to never fully recover. Maybe it was some physical ailment such as arthritis that had taken its toll and caused the man's hand to become useless in this current condition. At this point, it did not matter how it happened, when it happened or how long it had been this way. God was performing a miracle in response to the man's obedience. As the man stretched out his hand, can you imagine that finger by finger, the hand that was so bound by infirmity or affliction, became loosed? Finger after finger, joint after joint, muscle after muscle, that hand stretched out until it was completely extended! As the man stretched out his hand in obedience, *"his hand was restored"* (Mark 3:5)! Can you imagine the excitement in the building? Can you imagine the joy in that man's heart? He could take his name off the disability list! He could cancel his appointment at the soup kitchen! He could go home and hug his wife and stroke her face, with a brand-new hand! He could hold hands with his children or throw a ball and catch it with a restored hand! He could go to work and now make a living for himself and his family. Life would be completely different for this man after this experience with Jesus! Such is the case with any man and woman that would dare to stretch out their hand in obedience to God!

Whole As The Other

The Bible says that *"his hand was restored WHOLE AS THE OTHER"* (Mark 3:5). Friend, God does not do anything halfway. He does not do anything partially! When God does something, He finishes it. It may not be instantly. It may take some time but when He is done, it will be perfect! His withered hand was just as good as his other hand! One of these days, God is going to finish this work that He started in us. He is the *"Author and Finisher of our faith"* (Hebrews 12:2). Paul said that we could be *"confident of this very thing, that He which hath begun a good work in you will perform it until the day of Jesus Christ:"* (Philippians 1:6). There are a lot of days between the day that we got saved and the day that we will go to heaven. However, many of those days feel like nothing is happening. Some of those days we may feel like God has forgotten all about us, but He has not! He started that good work in you, and He is going to complete it one of these days! John said *"it doth not yet appear what we shall be: but we know that, when He shall appear, we shall be like Him; for we shall see Him as He is"* (1 John 3:2). Right now, God is working on us, piece by piece, making us more like Jesus. He is restoring every part of our broken life until it reflects the beauty of His grace and the fullness of His love but one of these days the work will be done and EVERY PART of us will look just like Him!

Isn't that worth stretching for? To know that we are a work in progress but one day the project will be complete, and the finished product will be Christ revealed through us! We can and will experience this transforming work, one area at a time, if we can SURVIVE THE STRETCHING!!!

A Last Word

In August of 2018, I was pastoring the Friendfield PH Church when the Lord showed me a wonderful vision. It was a cloudy, overcast day and as I was walking that morning, the Lord began to speak to me. Iwas walking on Friendfield Road, heading back towardthe Church, when I felt the Lord say, "Look up." When I did, I saw a cloud over the Church that looked like aman's hand balled up in a fist. I could see big drops of water falling through the fingers. The Lord spoke to me and said, "My Hand has never left Friendfield and what you are experiencing right now is just a little drop at a time." We were having some good services at Friendfield and the Presence of the Lord was manifesting, and souls were being saved and uplifted! The Lord was showing me that those were just drops of blessings that He allowed to fall on the Church. That morning, as I turned the corner and could see the Church in full view with that Hand just over it in the clouds, something happened that I could almost feel the ground shake! I could see that Hand turn loose and water began to fall onto Friendfield Church like a waterfall! God again spoke to me and said, "If the people of Friendfield will stretch their hand toward me, I will stretch My Hand toward them!" I could see that life-giving water flowing from the Hand of God onto Friendfield Church! Friendfield was a solid Church that loved the Lord and had a firm foundation on the Word of God, but they had been through some dry times. They had been through some hurting times. In all of that, God had not removed His hand from them. At this season, He was wanting to pour out this refreshing water and He did! He went on to say "When the water begins to flow, it is going to flow to Pamplico, Johnsonville, Lake City, Scranton and Coward. It is going to touch every area of this community." And God did just that! Over the next year, we had folks added to our Church from all five of those neighboring communities and God did a work that refreshed and strengthened the church.

Why am I telling you this and how does this apply to you? More than likely, you do not attend the Friendfield PH Church. You may have never even heard of it but God is no respecter of persons! (See Acts 10:34). What God did and wanted to do at Friendfield, He wants to do and is able to do for every Bible believing child of God! Do you want to experience more of God? Do you want the refreshing water of the Holy Ghost poured out on your life until it flows to every member of your home, family and community? God wants to do so much more than we could ever expect but we have to be willing to stretch our hand to Him! When we do, He is past ready to stretch His Hand out to us! Keep on Believing! Keep on Praying! Keep on Stretching! God's blessings on you as you SURVIVE THE STRETCHING and experience all that God has for you!

Made in the USA
Middletown, DE
01 April 2024

52263401R00076